SMP 11-16

Teacher's guide to Books
A1, A2 and A3

CAMBRIDGE
UNIVERSITY PRESS

Published by the Press Syndicate of the University of Cambridge

The Pitt Building, Trumpington Street, Cambridge CB2 1RP

40 West 20th Street, New York, NY 10011-4211, USA

10 Stamford Road, Oakleigh, Melbourne 3166, Australia

© Cambridge University Press 1995

First published 1995

Printed in Great Britain by Scotprint Ltd, Musselburgh

A catalogue record for this book is available from the British Library

ISBN 0 521 44882 4 paperback

Contents

The School Mathematics Project was founded in 1961 with the aim of improving the teaching of mathematics in schools. SMP authors are experienced teachers and each new venture is tested in draft by schools before publication.

Books A1, A2 and *A3* and this teacher's guide have been written by

Philippa Barr	Sue Karwowski
Debbie Sanderson	Cathryn Mackintosh
Rose Griffiths	Paul Scruton

The writing team has been led by Paul Scruton.

Certain chapters are based on work done by Geoff Fowler, Hilary Gill, Peter Gostling, Liz Jones, John Perry, Alison Pike, Rob Powell, John Sharples, Mary-Lou Wheeler and Eddie Wilde.

The authors' warm thanks go to the teachers who tested the draft materials in their schools and to SMP staff who made helpful comments on them, in particular Bob Hartman, Elizabeth Jackson, Peter Ransom, Janet Sheaf and Jo Waddingham. Others, notably Pam Keetch and Nichola Lake, gave first-class administrative support. Sue Kearsey provided valuable horticultural advice. The authors are also grateful to those at Cambridge University Press who worked on these books, particularly Angela Ashton, Richard Bailey and Rosemary Tennison, whose encouragement, creativity and painstaking commitment have been indispensable.

The authors and publisher wish to thank the pupils and staff of Littleover Community School, Derby for their help in connection with this teacher's guide, and the Brown family for permission to use the photograph on page 95.

Introduction

The Amber series is for low-attaining 13- to 16-year-olds (years 9–11 in England and Wales, years 10–12 in Northern Ireland and S2–S4 in Scotland). It is intended to be suitable for all schools, whether or not they use SMP 11–16; in particular, we do not assume that the SMP 11–16 booklet scheme has been used in the preceding two years.

The pupil's *Books A1* to *A9* are in three groups of three. Each group of three books is accompanied by a pack of worksheet masters and a teacher's guide like this one. Very roughly, each group can be regarded as a year's work.

The teacher's guides are an essential component of the course. In them we first give general advice on the needs of low attainers and strategies for teaching and planning. Then we provide classroom notes for each chapter on

- the mathematics that is being taught and the skills and concepts that are required
- teacher-led activities that highlight the mathematical ideas
- teacher-led discussion of what pupils see and read on the page
- points at which the teacher should check that pupils have understood key ideas
- suggestions for support, extra practice and extension work

The symbol ◆T▶ appears in the pupil's book where teacher's input is particularly needed, either to lead an activity or discussion or to carry out a check. Advice on how to make the input is marked with the same symbol at the corresponding point in the teacher's guide.

We are conscious of wide variation in the experience of those reading this guide: some special needs teachers feel very confident about the mathematical aspect of their work, others less so; equally, mathematics specialists differ in their experience and resourcefulness when it comes to teaching low attainers. Whatever your experience and interest we want to help you gain professional satisfaction from helping low attainers with their mathematics even though their needs can sometimes seem daunting. If, in trying to support as many teachers as possible, we occasionally state what to you is the obvious, we apologise now.

Who are 'low attainers'?

In terms of the existing SMP 11–16 clientele, the Amber series has been developed for pupils for whom the Green series is too hard (and for them it can form the basis of a complete mathematics curriculum) and those who are doing an appreciable amount of work from the Green series but who need support in some areas of that work.

In practice, though, low attainers do not form a uniform group. Denvir, Stolz and Brown (1) categorised possible causes of low attainment as:

physical, physiological or sensory defects;

emotional or behavioural problems;

impaired performance due to physical causes,
    such as tiredness, drugs, general ill-health;

attitude: anxiety; lack of motivation;

inappropriate teaching;

too many changes of teachers, lack of continuity;

general slowness in grasping ideas;

cultural differences, English not first language;

impoverished home background;

difficulty in oral expression or in written work;

poor reading ability;

gaps in education, absence from school, frequent
    transfer from one school to another;

immaturity, late development, youngest in the year group;

low self-concept leading to lack of self-confidence.

The authors comment that several of these causes are beyond the control of the school and that, because they can exist in combination, 'the nature of each pupil's low attainment will be highly idiosyncratic and possibly unique'. This is a disheartening analysis; but you shouldn't conclude that since you cannot overcome all these difficulties you cannot help with any of them. On the contrary, as the teacher, you can achieve a great deal if you recognise your own central role in identifying and meeting needs: you can adapt content and the way it is presented, you can give pupils opportunities to speak, listen, observe and draw, as well as to read and write, and you can provide the enthusiasm, reassurance and praise that are essential if they are to make progress. The Amber books play their part by being supportive and coherent, but they cannot offer what only a teacher can provide; most emphatically, they are *not* for pupils to be left to work through on their own.

Denvir, Stolz and Brown also point out that there are 'two groups of low attainers – those who are likely to "catch up" and those who are not'; but since we cannot be sure into which of these two categories a particular pupil will eventually fall the provision that is made will have to be temporary for some and long-term for others. It is also true that low attainers often have specific strengths that have gone unrecognised because of their more general learning difficulties. Don't be afraid to try things: they may sometimes reveal a surprising measure of talent. With these points in mind, the teacher's guides often suggest other work for when pupils have succeeded with a piece of work in Amber – classroom activities for extra practice or challenge, or related work from the Green series or Resource packs for use at a later date. (A note on the Green series and resource packs is provided on page 18 for teachers who may be unfamiliar with them.)

Broadening the learning experience

The special needs of low attainers usually range wider than mathematics: the difficulties that they encounter in the mathematics classroom may well be typical of those they experience in other subjects – lack of confidence, problems of concentration, extreme difficulty in relating pieces of information or ideas to one another. We regard helping pupils with their mathematics as a way of helping meet their broader needs, not as an end in itself isolated from their general educational and social development. Low attainers benefit from a sense of social cohesion, and we have tried to support this need by using games and other group activities as vehicles for learning. They also benefit from the reinforcement that can be achieved through collaborative work between subject departments: several of the Amber chapters are cross-curricular in nature and we hope that they will encourage helpful co-operation of this kind.

The pupil's and teacher's books include many activities that encourage practical skills. It is tempting to skip over these (especially if you do not have your own permanent teaching base), regarding them as optional extras. But it is important not to do so. They all have a definite mathematical purpose and have been found to stimulate pupil's interest. Several of them make links with art, a subject which many pupils enjoy. Such activities will involve you in a certain amount of preparation but we have done all we can to simplify the requirements and set them out for you in the 'Before you start' sections of the classroom notes. A general equipment list for *Books A1, A2* and *A3* is also given on pages 16–17.

Providing the opportunity to learn

It is often quite difficult to set suitable targets for current learning. Brown and Onion (2) provide a useful insight when they state that 'learning takes place at the borders of students' understanding'. A simple diagram helps illustrate the point.

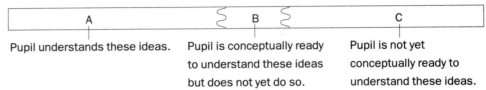

Area A is what the pupil understands. Some of these concepts and skills may need practice, but they should not need to be *taught* again. If we try to reteach them we are wasting time, ours and the pupils'.

On the other hand, the concepts in area C are not likely to be understood for quite some time, after a lot of other supporting ideas are in place. You may be able to help pupils complete work from that area, but real learning will not have occurred. Resources will again be wasted if pupils spend a significant amount of time failing on, or being coaxed through, work that is plainly too difficult for them.

Area B represents ideas at the 'borders of students' understanding', where learning can begin and where your teaching skills need to be focussed. Locating that area for a particular pupil is a central aim of diagnostic work. The key idea is that of *backtracking*: when the pupil has not understood an idea or our attempt to explain it we often need to go backwards until we reach a point that is clearly within the pupil's understanding and teach from there. This takes experience, but some simple dos and don'ts may help. Let us suppose that a pupil – let's call her Sharon – is stuck with a piece of written work …

- Start by asking and listening. Avoid the temptation just to say 'You do them like this …'
- Ask her to tell you what she has done so far. This should give you a picture of what she can do in this topic (her area A). It may also help her draw together the threads of recent work on which the present task may depend (in case the problem is failure of short term memory or lack of concentration, or not expecting to have to organise recent ideas in this way). Note any concepts that she seems confident about and her ways of expressing them. You may be able to word your eventual explanations in similar terms.

- Ask her to read you the question that is causing the problem, or whether she would like you to read it to her. This is partly to check whether the problem is one of literacy. Wait for a while to see whether rereading has given her any ideas.

- Ask her to tell you what the problem is asking. Having to express the problem in her own words may again help Sharon organise her own thoughts and again may help you pinpoint some of the problems.

- If rereading and re-expressing the question don't do the trick, think of simpler related problems. Talk about a more concrete version of the task: if the question is about money ask about coins; if the question is about counting numbers talk about objects that the numbers may be counting. If this doesn't seem to work, ask her to get coins or objects and see if handling them helps her answer the question.

- Think of simple ways of building confidence – providing rough paper or a calculator, suggesting that she works in pencil instead of pen at this stage.

- Be encouraging and use praise when Sharon makes small steps in the right direction, especially when she would not otherwise realise she is making progress.

- The needs of the pupil come first, not the material. The objective is that Sharon learns something, not that you and she struggle to the end of a particular Amber chapter.

- Don't try to put right here and now all the problems you have discovered. Sharon will need to move forward from the work she has been doing today, but if you try to do too much before she has time to consolidate ideas and you have time to plan ahead you may find that she is soon adrift again.

- Make a brief note of what the problems were and the progress you made. Record keeping that reminds you of work you need to do with the pupil in the future is *the most useful kind*.

Throughout the work, encourage pupils to take some responsibility for establishing what they can do and telling you about their areas of difficulty. This can prevent you from pressing on too far – though sometimes, given the chance to tell you, pupils will surprise you with how far they are ready to go.

Giving practice

Practising skills is important: 'little and often' is the key. There also needs to be a good balance between familiar forms of practice (which help pupils feel secure) and practice that varies in style and context (so that they can see what they are practising *for*). In this way you can help forestall the contrasting complaints that 'we've done this all before' and that 'it isn't maths' (because it isn't just a page of sums).

While using the Amber course you can provide practice in broadly five forms.

- Practice and revision built into the pupils' books
- Repeated use of some of the games
- Teacher-led practice activities
- The review sections
- The 'Time to remember' pages

Practice and revision built into the pupils' books

Where appropriate, we have included practice with familiar concepts and skills within work designed to teach the pupil new ones. Of course, a particular piece of work may be practice for one pupil but a learning experience for another. If it is practice, it may be safe to let the pupil work alone. But if learning needs to take place you should be ready to lead discussion, ask questions, set small challenges and provide support.

We have also tried to use vivid images, ideas and activities that your pupils will remember when you refer to them again in revision sessions.

Repeated use of games

All the games have a serious purpose, usually involving a mix of strategic skill and number practice, with the need to maintain the game's pace motivating the use of mental calculation. Games are also self-checking· they give pupils an incentive to make sure that their opponents' arithmetic is right! It is easy to assume that a game should be played once and then not again for fear of wasting time. But that needn't be the case. If pupils have particularly enjoyed a game this may be partly from the pleasure of having to keep up a new skill. It is worth watching to see whether this is the case. If so, the skill will almost certainly be reinforced if they have another go at the game in a few weeks' time. You could also include occasional sessions in which pupils are free to choose a game that they have enjoyed or felt particularly challenged by in the past. Encourage pupils to become aware of how much better or quicker they are becoming in repeated playing of games either by recording how their scores improve or by timing themselves.

Using the Reviews

There are five review sections at the end of each of *Books A1, A2* and *A3*. They sample successive (though sometimes overlapping) sections of the book (indicated by page numbers), and after *Book A1* they also refer back to earlier books. They are intended as medium- to long-term revision, to be done at least a couple of weeks after the relevant pages, *not* as immediate follow-up to each chapter.

Using the 'Time to remember' pages

At the back of each book, there is a 'Time to remember' page. This consists of key mathematical words, grouped by topics, and a few visual reminders. The page is best used when pupils are well through the work in the book: they can use it as a handy memory aid or a vocabulary list to check spellings; or you can base a discussion around it, asking pupils to tell you about work in which they saw particular words used.

Practising and developing number skills

Nowhere is practice more important than with number skills. Although the books offer varied work on reading and writing numbers, pupils also need to hear numbers used, to 'think on their feet about numbers' and to say numbers.

One approach, endorsed by Brown and Onion, is the use of 'count-round games', in which pupils take it in turns to recite the next number in a sequence defined by the teacher (such as 'Up from 85 in ones' or 'Down from 100 in tens'):

> They are very simple for students to understand, which helps them to feel confident... They are ideal at the start of a lesson to put students at their ease. They are also a shared activity, so can be used to help to develop a sense of cohesion within the group making them particularly appropriate for a small remedial group who have been withdrawn from their friends in the main maths lesson.

It is best to do only one count-round game in a lesson, and it may be a good idea to return to it at the end of lesson as reinforcement. Count-round games needn't be restricted to pure numbers: you can also use them to practise time or other measures. In the classroom notes we suggest some count-round games that you can use with particular pieces of work, but you can easily think up your own.

Confidence with numbers can also be established and reinforced by number games played in small groups. For this purpose we recommend *Count me in* (Mosley and Lutrario (3)), a package which includes a pack of 0–100 cards, 23 'game-cards' – each describing a game to be played using the 0–100 cards – and a teacher's book. Written for primary children, the game-cards are rather young-looking, but the games have been used effectively with older low attaining pupils and there is no reason why you should not explain the instructions for them yourself. The teacher's book contains special sections on second language learners, children with physical handicaps, deaf and partially hearing children, and blind and partially sighted children.

It is important that pupils become confident with number facts. The number work in the books provides support for steady progression in this respect, but it is essential that it is reinforced by teacher-led number practice. The use of multiplication facts broadly follows this sequence.

Book A1

×	0	1	2	3	4	5	6	7	8	9	10
1	0	1	2	3	4	5	6	7	8	9	10
2	0	2	4	6	8	10					20
3	0	3	6	9	12	15					30
4	0	4	8	12	16	20					40
5	0	5	10	15	20	25	30	35	40	45	50
6	0	6				30					60
7	0	7				35					70
8	0	8				40					80
9	0	9				45					90
10	0	10	20	30	40	50	60	70	80	90	100

Book A2

×	0	1	2	3	4	5	6	7	8	9	10
1	0	1	2	3	4	5	6	7	8	9	10
2	0	2	4	6	8	10	12	14	16	18	20
3	0	3	6	9	12	15	18	21	24	27	30
4	0	4	8	12	16	20					40
5	0	5	10	15	20	25	30	35	40	45	50
6	0	6	12	18		30					60
7	0	7	14	21		35					70
8	0	8	16	24		40					80
9	0	9	18	27		45					90
10	0	10	20	30	40	50	60	70	80	90	100

We give other details about progression in the number work within the classroom notes.

Although 'mental' number skills and pencil-and-paper working are important, we have assumed that a simple calculator is available throughout the course, and one of our aims is that pupils should increase their confidence in using it. We also want pupils to come to judge for themselves when a calculator, or some other method, is the most efficient way of working something out. For this reason we have not used 'calculator permitted' or 'calculator prohibited' icons, though illustrations occasionally hint at the method we would expect to be used. Judging between methods of calculation does not come easily (even the most numerate of us occasionally work out trivial things on calculators or use pencil and paper when a calculator would be more efficient), so you should be ready to guide pupils, encouraging them to discuss their choice of method.

Measures

We include a considerable amount of work on quantities such as length, weight, time and eventually capacity, and the various units in which they are measured. The emphasis for low attainers must be on understanding how to measure rather than the manipulation of the quantities as pure numbers. For this reason it is essential that pupils use a range of instruments – different sorts of rulers and tape measures, various kinds of scales and a range of clocks and watches – in practical activities linked to the chapters.

The ability to approximate and estimate can really only be developed gradually through discussion and practical work on measures. Look for opportunities to ask 'about how much…?', 'how long do you think…?', 'about how tall…?, 'about how heavy…?'; and encourage pupils to look at their answers and decide whether they are sensible.

Using language

Like anyone else, the low attainer will find it much easier to give an oral response to a question than a written one. For this reason, it is often a good idea to start a new topic with a teacher-led question and answer session: it can start ideas flowing faster and more freely than when every response has to be dispiritingly committed to paper. Written work is important but care needs to be taken that it doesn't degenerate into short answers which, apart from attracting your row of ticks, amount to little as a piece of communication.

Our aim of helping meet low attainers' broader needs includes giving them supportive opportunities for reading. While we have tried to make the language as clear and simple as possible there will obviously be some pupils with extreme reading difficulties who need extra help. Sometimes, too, it is impossible to lower the language level beyond a certain point without limiting the work or creating ambiguity. The rules for games are an obvious example: they are always harder to read than to play by; but rather than relegate them to the teacher's guide, we have usually left them in the pupil's text, recognising that you (or a neighbouring pupil) will often need to help interpret them.

Developing classroom skills, clarifying classroom ground rules

Low attainers may never have learnt the classroom procedures that most children grasp early in their school careers and which secondary school teachers usually take for granted. They may not know the conventions for following work on the page of a textbook, may not see the value of writing down working to help keep track of their thoughts, may not appreciate the need to number their written answers or even to write them down at all! Some may not appreciate the customs and courtesies of playing games (dealing out cards, deciding fairly who goes first). They may also be unsure about your ground rules for mathematics lessons: are they expected to help themselves to a worksheet when they see it mentioned, or equipment if they think they need it? What should they do when they finish a piece of work? How are they expected to keep their bits and pieces – finished and unfinished worksheets, sets of cards for unfinished games – together between lessons? And when and how are they expected to ask for help?

Such skills and ground rules need teaching and clarifying. But choose a time to do this when the mathematical demands are moderate. And remember too that just like so many other things you will need to come back to these routines and practise them. The time will be well invested: pupils stand to gain confidence in organising and getting on with their mathematics while acquiring skills of general educational value; and some of your time tied up in sorting out minor organisational problems should be released for teaching.

Managing the pupils' work and your own time

You may have had mixed feelings about our advice earlier on diagnosing problems. 'It's all very well in theory', you may have thought, 'but there isn't time for it in a real classroom with a group the size I have to teach.' Of course you need to be realistic about what you can achieve, but we believe teaching of this kind is possible if certain strategies are employed to help release time.

- Delegate to members of the class organisational tasks such as getting out and checking in equipment. With low attainers, start this in a small way until they get to know what their tasks are; then gradually increase your expectations.

- Sequence the work to suit pupils' needs. The Amber chapters have been put in an order that we think will give variety and allow progression. But you do not need to keep to that order if you can see others that would be more effective.

- Plan stretches of work that are varied and are of a length that gives pupils a sense of satisfaction. Most Amber chapters are short. The longer ones allow you to see how a sequence of work develops, but some of them may work better if they are split into shorter sections with other work interspersed: this breaks up the work into manageable bites; it gives pupils variety; and it gives you a chance to look at their work, see where difficulties have arisen, and if necessary provide extra help before they go on to the next section. Consider dividing long lessons into sections, each in a different style – for example, short introductory teacher-led whole-class number practice, practical activities and written work.

- When planning your lessons, refer to the notes you made earlier from your diagnostic work. If they suggest that most of the class are ready to make progress with a certain topic, consider a class-teaching approach to it. If they indicate a topic that a few pupils need to concentrate on, consider gathering them together and teaching them as a small group. There is no point in individualising your approach if there are no individual needs.

- Of course, pupils will often need time devoted to them individually, and even teaching a subgroup presents the problem of what to do with the rest of the class. If in order to teach in this way you have to leave the rest only lightly supervised, give them something that is relatively 'sure-fire', with a significant amount of practice in it, so that you can be reasonably certain you will not be called away from your individual or small group during the time you have set aside for them.

- Ration your time with individuals. Try to get them started so that they can move ahead under their own steam, then come back later to see how they are getting on.

- Have 10- to 15-minute fillers ready – such as some of the games or puzzles – for when individual pupils finish work ahead of the others, or the whole class finishes well before the end of the lesson.

- Keep stocks of material and equipment tidy and topped up: there is nothing more frustrating than to have a well-planned lesson brought to a halt because a particular worksheet is out of stock.

The planner tables

To help you formulate your scheme of work we have provided a planner table for each book. That for *Book A1* is on pages 20–21, for *Book A2* on pages 48–49 and for *Book A3* on pages 78–79.

The first column of each table lists the chapters with a short summary of each.

The next column lists the worksheets for the chapter. Fuller details about reproducing the worksheets are given in the reprographics guide on pages 13–15.

Next we show links with later chapters in Amber: these show you where the work is leading and may help you when trying to fill gaps caused by a pupil's absence. (In cases where a particular chapter crucially depends on competence with work in an earlier chapter we point this out in the classroom notes.)

Next we list some items in the Green series and *Resource packs A, B* and *C* that pupils can do if they have done well in an Amber chapter. We don't intend these to be done straight away: it will usually be much better if a period of time is allowed to elapse so that this follow-up work forms part of a process of consolidation. Those Amber topics that are not covered in the Green series may form a useful supplement for pupils following Green and where this is the case we give details in this column.

A further column lists software that we recommend for use with some chapters.

The final columns give approximate level references with respect to the national curriculum for England and Wales, the common curriculum for Northern Ireland, and the Scottish 5–14 guidelines. These are included less for the purpose of producing a scheme of work (with low attainers there is no substitute for planning based on the sorts of diagnostic procedures outlined on pages 4–5) than to provide guidance in the event that you are required to link the work to levels for some official purpose.

Reprographics guide

The table on the next two pages gives detailed guidance on reproducing worksheets, sets of cards and OHP slides from the *Worksheet masters for Books A1, A2 and A3* (ISBN 0 521 47841 3). If you are fortunate enough to have someone to do the copying for you, it should be possible simply to hand over this table rather than give detailed instructions yourself (but see the remarks below about the quantity guide).

Back to back

As an economy measure, it is sometimes possible to copy two worksheets on to a sheet of paper, one on each side. The first column shows pairs of sheets that can be treated this way bracketed together.

One side only

These cannot be backed: some, for example, have to be cut up.

Reproduce on material other than paper

Photocopying onto acetate is a way of making some very cheap learning aids and some effective OHP slides. But you must use the special A4 sheets of acetate designed to be put through a photocopier. You can get them from good commercial stationers or educational suppliers.

Reusable

If you can have the reusable worksheets laminated it may be a cost-effective way of extending their life.

Quantity guide

This gives an idea of requirements for a group of ten pupils doing Amber. For a reusable item, this is a once-and-for-all requirement; otherwise it is the annual order. The figures are *rough*, however: actual quantities will depend on the extent to which you organise the work on an individualised or whole-class basis, particularly in the case of cards for games.

Size check

Where pupils are to measure from a worksheet, lengths on it must not be affected by distortion. Although the worksheet masters are printed to precise standards, factors like paper stretch can cause problems and photocopiers do not always reproduce exactly the same size. Where a size check is given, photocopy one sheet, check the relevant measurement and if necessary make an appropriate adjustment to the copier's zoom setting; then print the necessary quantity.

Reprographics guide

Reproduce on plain paper Back-to-back	One side only	Reproduce on material other than plain paper	Reusable	Quantity guide	Notes/size check
		A1–OHP1 acetate	✓		1 per teacher
		A1–1 coloured card	✓	10	Each set on different coloured card
A1–2			✓	10	
		A1–3 acetate	✓	2	
A1–4			✗	10	
A1–5			✗	10	
		A1–OHP2 acetate	✓		1 per teacher
A1–6			✗	10	
A1–7			✗	10	
		A1–8 white card	✗	10	
		A1–9 white card	✗	10	
		A1–10 coloured card	✓	10	Each set on different coloured card
A1–11			✓	10	
A1–12			✗	10	
A1–13			✗	10	
A1–14			✗	10	
		A1–15 coloured card	✓	5	Each set on different coloured card
		A1–OHP3 acetate	✓		1 per teacher
		A1–16 card	✓	4	
		A1–17 card	✓	4	
A1–18			✗	10	
	A1–19		✗	10	
A1–20			✗	10	
	A1–21		✗	10	
A1–22			✗	10	
	A2–1		✗	10	The top square should be 80mm x 80mm.
	A2–2		✗	10	The top square should be 90mm x 90mm.
		A2–3 coloured card	✓	5	Each set on different coloured card
		A2–4 coloured card	✓	5	Each set on different coloured card
A2–5			✗	10	
A2–6			✗	10	
	A2–7		✗	10	
	A2–8		✗	10	
	A2–9		✗	10	
		A2–10 coloured card	✓	5	Together the three worksheets make
		A2–11 coloured card	✓	5	a set of cards. Each set should be
		A2–12 coloured card	✓	5	in a different colour.
		A2–13 acetate	✓	2	
A2–14			✗	10	
		A2–OHP1 acetate	✓		1 per teacher
	A2–15		✗	10	
A2–16			✗	10	

Reproduce on plain paper		Reproduce on material other than plain paper	Reusable	Quantity guide	Notes/size check
Back-to-back	One side only				
	A2–17		✗	10	
	A2–18		✗	10	
		A2–19 coloured card	✓	2	} Together the two worksheets make a set of cards. Each set should be in a different colour.
		A2–20 coloured card	✓	2	
		A2–21 coloured card	✓	3	Each set on different coloured card
	A2–22		✗	10	The square should be 160mm x 160mm.
	A2–23		✓	4	
	A2–24		✗	10	The square should be 140mm x 140mm.
	A2–25		✗	10	
	A2–26		✗	10	
		A2–27 card	✓	3	
		A2–28 card	✓	3	
		A2–29 card	✓	3	
		A2–30 card	✓	3	
A3–1			✗	10	The scissors should be 143mm long.
A3–2			✗	10	The long bulldog clip should be 141mm long.
A3–3			✗	10	The scissors should be 143mm long.
A3–4			✗	10	The long bulldog clip should be 141mm long.
		A3–OHP1 acetate	✓		1 per teacher
	A3–5		✗	10	
A3–6			✗	10 x 2	Reproduce worksheet on both sides of paper
	A3–7		✓	2	Enlarge to A3 if possible
		A3–8 buff or peach paper	✓	10	
		A3–OHP2 acetate	✓		1 per teacher
		A3–9 blue card	✓	2	
		A3–10 green card	✓	2	
		A3–11 yellow card	✓	2	
	A3–12		✗	5	
		A3–13 card	✓	2	Each set a different colour
A3–14			✗	10	
A3–15			✗	10	
A3–16			✗	10	
A3–17			✗	10	
A3–18			✗	10	
A3–19			✗	10	
		A3–OHP3 acetate	✓		1 per teacher

Equipment list for Books A1, A2 and A3

This list gives approximate quantities of equipment needed for a group of 10 pupils. It assumes whole-group teaching but some sharing of equipment has been allowed for. If you are using some of the chapters with larger Green groups you will need to increase some quantities accordingly. We assume that basic four-function calculators and the usual range of classroom stationery are available.

The SMP learning aids may be purchased from Cambridge University Press. Other items of equipment may be obtained form Tarquin Publications (Stradbroke, Diss, Norfolk IP21 5JP), NES Arnold (Ludlow Hill Road, West Bridgford, Nottingham NG2 6HD), Hope Education Limited (Orb Mill, Huddersfield Road, Waterhead, Oldham, Lancashire OL4 2ST) and Invicta Plastics (Oadby, Leicestershire LE2 4LB).

SMP learning aids

Pie chart scales (pack of 10 scales) 1 pack ISBN 0 521 26366 2
Angle measurers (pack of 5 measurers) 2 packs ISBN 0 521 25435 3
(Possibly) punched strips (1 set of 12) 1 pack ISBN 0 521 25436 1

Equipment from suppliers other than CUP

5 plastic mirrors, preferably at least 10 cm by 5 cm
5 dice numbered 1–6
Up to 10 dice numbered 0–5
5 eight-sided dice (see below)
Up to about 100 counters
A generous supply of multilink (or similar) cubes
5 Triman safety compasses, which we recommend for
    drawing circles in preference to the type with a point.
About £100 in plastic token pound coins

Items to be collected or prepared

Elastic
5 dice marked A to F
5 eight-sided dice marked N, S, E, W, NE, NW, SE, SW
1 or more packs of playing cards
Square coloured gummed paper or origami paper
A table tennis ball or marble
A spirit level
A beaker of the kind used in science
A piece of string about 2 metres long and a heavy nut

A pile of old newspapers

Various rulers measuring in centimetres, millimetres and inches, a metre rule (more than one, with different styles of marking if possible) and various measuring tapes

Kitchen scales, bathroom scales and, if possible, other sorts of weighing scales

A clock or watch that works; a disused clock which can be used to show how its hands turn

A set of Scrabble for possible follow-up work

Recipe books or cards

5 copies of a street map of the local neighbourhood

Real coins from time to time and at one stage in *Book A3* a £20 note, a £10 note and a £5 note

Adhesive label or masking tape

Filter paper or cut out circles

Paper fasteners (for punched strips)

(Possibly) large wall-hanging calendar

(Possibly) seed merchants' catalogues

(Possibly) collection of devices for measuring right-angles

Formal assessment

Appropriate assessment of pupils can be both informative and motivating. The SMP Graduated Assessment Profile of Mathematical Achievement has been developed by the SMP and the Oxford and Cambridge Schools Examination Board for use alongside pupils' normal classroom work. The Profile is available to pupils aged 13 to 16 and includes an Amber band. It comprises items that test written, mental, practical and oral skills, and which are grouped into Stages. As soon as a pupil reaches the required standard on (say) Amber Stage One, the school can present the official Amber Stage One certificate.

Further details of the Profile may be obtained by writing to

SMP Graduated Assessment
Oxford and Cambridge Schools Examination Board
Purbeck House
Purbeck Road
Cambridge CB2 2PU

The SMP 11–16 Green series and Resource packs A, B and C

The Green series consists of *Books G1* to *G9*, with a further book, *G+*, for use throughout the series; together they cover the whole of the national curriculum for England and Wales (and the common curriculum for Northern Ireland) up to level 5 and the Foundation level of the Scottish Certificate of Education, Standard Grade. The Green materials reflect the view that the pupils for whom they are designed need a wide variety of presentation, content and method of working in their mathematics.

Resource packs A, B and *C* are collections of 32 cards containing varied activities, including drawing and making work, games, puzzles and investigations. They may be used by individuals, pairs or groups. Respectively, their ISBNs are: 0 521 30124 6, 0 521 31457 7 and 0 521 31003 2.

References

(1) Brenda Denvir, Chris Stolz and Margaret Brown, *Low attainers in mathematics 5–16: policies and practices in schools*, Methuen Educational 1982

(2) Julia Brown and Alice Onion, *The mathematics teachers' development series, Pack 2: Low attainers and the national curriculum*, Framework Press, St Leonard's House, St Leonardgate, Lancaster LA1 1NN

(3) Fran Mosley and Christopher Lutrario, *Count me in*, Harcourt Brace Jovanovich 1990

Book A1

Most pupils (not just low attainers) value the opportunity to move on to fresh material, and this first book in the Amber series aims to provide an enjoyable start to a new course. We hope it will also give you the chance to offer an approach to mathematics that appeals to the pupils and helps you get to know them and their needs.

Many of the chapters in this book are designed to be introduced by the teacher. This allows you to get some initial feedback on how each topic is likely to be received and helps those pupils whose reading skills might otherwise prevent them from getting started. It also allows valuable discussion and practical work to take place.

Mathematical themes in this book

Work on shape and space is developed in **Left and right**, **Compass directions**, **Symmetrical letters and masks** and **Map grids**; a common thread is that of describing positions systematically.

Running through the number work is the idea of making up groups of five and ten and handling multiples of those numbers (the early questions in **Raffle**, **5s with hexagons**, the tally charts in **Toast and tallies**, **10s with triangles**, **Car boot sale** – where the amounts of money are multiples of 5p – and **10s on a grid**). This is an important aspect of our counting and money systems, so you will need to come back to it in class discussion alongside and between these chapters.

In this book we expect some knowledge of multiplication facts up to 5×5 and the ability to cope with multiples of 5p and 10p (though with coins available for support). Pupils may use their calculator for multiplications beyond these.

Work on money is developed carefully: **Raffle**, **Toast and tallies** and **Chocolate boxes** all contain short pieces of money work that should allow you to identify problems before the weightier **Car boot sale** is attempted.

All pupils need to appreciate how statistical information is collected, processed and presented. **Toast and tallies** makes a confident start in dealing with bias, and efficiency in carrying out surveys.

Planner table for Book A1 (see p.12)

Page	Chapter	Worksheets (see pp.13–15)	Links with later work in Amber
4	**Left and right** Describing left and right from different viewpoints	A1–OHP1	
12	**Raffle** Multiples of 5p and numbers in words and figures		A1 p.32 **Car boot sale**
13	**5s with hexagons** Game about pairing numbers that add up to 5	A1–1 A1–2	A1 p.30 **10s with triangles**
14	**Compass directions** Stating and following points of the compass	A1–3 A1–4 A1–5 A1–OHP2	
18	**Newsagent** Multiplication and addition of small amounts of money		A1 p.32 **Car boot sale**
19	**Toast and tallies** Making surveys purposeful, efficient and unbiased		
24	**Pinball wizard** Adding-on of numbers less than 20	A1–6	
25	**Symmetrical letters and masks** Making attractive symmetrical designs with a vertical line of symmetry	A1–7 A1–8 A1–9	A2 p.29 **Patterns by folding and cutting**
30	**10s with triangles** Game about pairing numbers that add up to 10	A1–10 A1–11	A1 p.37 **10s on a grid**
31	**Chocolate boxes** Adding small amounts of money	A1–12 A1–13	A1 p.32 **Car boot sale**
32	**Car boot sale** Getting the total cost of purchases and giving change		A2 p.35 **Going halves**
36	**Cubes in a mirror** Identifying mirror images in three dimensions		
37	**10s on a grid** Game about finding groups of numbers that add up to 10	A1–14	
38	**Map grids** Map coordinates labelling squares and use of a street index	A1–15 A1–OHP3	
42	**Early starters** Diagnostic work on telling the time	A1–16 A1–17	A2 p.7 **Getting it taped** A2 p.24 **Clock watching**
44	**Review: pages 4 to 12**		
45	**Review: pages 13 to 23**	A1–18	
46	**Review: pages 14 to 29**	A1–19	
47	**Review: pages 30 to 36**	A1–20 A1–21	
48	**Review: pages 37 to 43**	A1–22	

Links with work in Green and Resource packs	Recommended software	England and Wales	Northern Ireland	Scotland
		National references		
G2 p.57 **Review: directions**		AT3 level 2	ATS level 2	Position and movement levels A,B,C, etc.
	Guess and **Boxes** in SMILE: The first 30 give practice in ordering whole numbers between 1 and 100	AT2 level 3	ATN level 3	Money level A Add and subtract level B Multiply and divide level B
		AT2 level 2	ATN level 2	Add and subtract level A
Can be used as a supplement for pupils following Green. G2 p.57 **Review: directions**	**Directions** on ECL disk 5 (The Woodstock Centre, Leicestershire): the pupil uses compass directions and distances as commands in this arcade-style game.	AT3 level 2	ATS level 4	Position and movement levels B,D
		AT2 level 3	ATN level 2	Add and subtract level B Multiply and divide level B
Can be used as a supplement for pupils following Green. G1 p.39 **Dice** G1 p.48 **Detective dice**		AT4 level 2	ATD level 2	Collect levels A,B,C Organise levels A,B,C Interpret levels A, B
		AT2 level 2	ATN level 2	Add and subtract level B
G1 p.22 **Review: reflection** G2 p.39 **Review: reflection**		AT3 level 3	ATS level 3	Symmetry levels B, C
		AT2 level 2	ATN level 2	Add and subtract level A
		AT2 level 2	ATN level 2	Add and subtract level B
G1 p.14 **Money** G1 p.20 **Money games**		AT2 level 3	ATN level 3 ATM level 2	Add and subtract level B Multiply and divide level B Money level B
		AT3 level 3	ATS level 4	Symmetry
Resource pack B card 14 'Number noughts and crosses' in **Noughts and...**		AT2 level 2	ATN level 2	Add and subtract level A
Can be used as supplement for pupils following Green.				Position and movement level B
Can be used as a supplement for pupils following Green who have difficulty telling the time. G1 p.32 **Time**		AT3 level 3	ATM level 2	Time levels A, B
	Line up in Straker 5 and the lowest level of **Carnival** in 10 out of 10 give practice in single digit addition and link with worksheets A1–18 and A1–20.			
Resource pack A card 20 **Arithmogons** Resource pack A card 22 **Stamps**				

Page 4 # Left and right

Links with *Book G2* p.57 **Review: directions**

The chapter aims to help pupils think about left and right from other points of view besides their own and to develop their ability to imagine themselves walking in a familiar environment. It begins with a section to check for individual difficulties with telling left from right and progresses towards a fairly demanding map reading activity. Along the way there are useful opportunities for discussion, as for example in judging the rights and wrongs of the car accident in section B.

Classroom organisation

There is no need to do all four sections in one go, especially as they are mostly teacher led. It may be better to divide the chapter and do other work in between. This will give you a chance to work on individual pupils' problems before going on to the later sections.

Before you start

You may need slide **A1–OHP1**.

A Parts of the body

Teacher-led activity

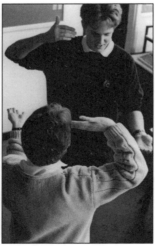

The following activity can be used to introduce the section or as a follow up to sort out any difficulties that arise from the work with the sports photos. You can do it with pupils working in pairs (one acting as the 'demonstrator' and the other as the 'copier') or with you demonstrating to one pupil or the whole class.

The demonstrator performs a physical act such as waving with the right hand. The copier has to perform the identical act (not the reflection of it). Use arm or leg movements singly to begin with but develop the activity by combining more than one movement as the pupil's competence develops.

If a pupil finds this too difficult, it may be useful to begin with the copier standing behind the demonstrator, only moving round into face-to-face position when confidence has been gained.

▶ **A1** The pupil's own answer

A2 Saima is right-handed.

A3 Linford Christie is carrying the Union Jack with his right hand.

A4 Pam Wright is resting her left hand on her thigh.

A5 Earvin Johnson is shooting with his right hand.

A6 Karen Smithies is going to land on her right foot.

A7 (a) The track line is on Katherine Merry's right-hand side.
(b) Her watch is on her left wrist.

A8 (a) Ian Botham is about to bowl with his right hand.
(b) His left elbow is bandaged.
(c) His right foot is on the ground.
(d) The stumps are on his right-hand side.

A9 Brian McClair is using his right foot.

A10 (a) Martin Dermott is carrying the ball with his left arm.
(b) He is holding off the French player's right shoulder.

A11 The white bandage is on the diver's left wrist.

A12 (a) The team badge is on the *player's* left.
(b) It is not possible to be sure.

Discussing the answers

This will give you the chance to ask further questions about left and right in the photographs (about how long is Pam Wright's putter in question **A4**? how high are the stumps in **A8**?). In **A12** how do we describe the sides of a piece of clothing – from the point of view of the wearer or from our point of view? And although the red player in the foreground is using only her left hand she may not be left handed since the standard grip involves having your left hand at the top of the stick, where hers is.

Checking and supporting

If difficulties arise you and the pupils can re-enact some of the photos (less energetically).

Some pupils (including very able ones) have difficulty distinguishing between left and right well into adulthood. But this is sometimes a problem about remembering which side is called which rather than an inability to change viewpoints mentally. Such people usually cope by making themselves remember that, for example, their right hand is the one they write with.

Page 10 **B Accident** Allow up to about an hour

Before you start
You may need slide **A1–OHP1.**

Leading the activity
The activity may be done by groups of three pupils, where one pupil is the cyclist, another is driving the white car and the third is driving the red car.

'It worked well: they took it further than I expected.'

A variant is to have a fourth person in each group – the judge – and to have a simplified trial: after hearing the 'evidence' from the three witnesses the judge has to decide who is guilty; you can then compare different groups' verdicts.

Alternatively, you may wish to divide the whole class into three groups, each representing one of the three road users, and run the activity as a whole class discussion. It may be easier to do this showing the slide **A1–OHP1**.

When we tested the activity we found that pupils did well in explaining the situation from their own point of view, but found writing about it much more difficult. However, it may well be worthwhile asking pupils to follow up with some writing about the page if you think they are capable of it.

Checking and supporting
If some pupils have difficulty you can set up a 'road junction' on a table and have model vehicles placed on it ready to make certain manoeuvres. They can then walk around the table and describe the situation from each vehicle's point of view.

Page 11 **C Imaginary walk** Allow 15 to 30 minutes

Leading the activity
You can do this activity with the whole class or a smaller group.

Tell the pupils to close their eyes. Tell them that you are going to give them some instructions for a walk around the school. They have to stay seated with their eyes closed and are to imagine that they are going on the walk.

Give them the instructions for the walk, starting from the classroom that they are now in. Allow a few seconds after each instruction for it to sink in. Use the words 'left' and 'right' and prompts like 'second door on the left'. You can occasionally mention a landmark: this will provide them with a check that they

'They liked "going in" doors that they are not allowed in, like the staff loos.'

are still 'with you'. Be careful: the pupils may know some parts of the school better than you do and will catch you out if you make a mistake. If you think they can cope with them, use phrases like 'about ten metres' occasionally. If your school is multi-storey, it is best to restrict the walk to one level, at least to start with.

When you have finished the walk tell the class to open their eyes and ask individual pupils where they think they have got to.

After you have done this a couple of times, arrange the class into pairs or small groups. In each case one pupil is to give the instructions while the other(s) go on the imaginary walk with their eyes closed. Alternatively you can have one pupil giving instructions to the whole class. At this stage you can tell pupils that they may ask questions if any of the instructions are not clear.

Once when we were trying this out a boy who was giving instructions to the class made a mistake part of the way through. The whole class ended up in the same place, but it was not the one he thought he had taken them to. He was amazed by this: it made him far more aware of the need to give precise instructions than any amount of telling by his teacher.

 ## D How well do you know your neighbourhood?

Before you start
Each pair will need a local map with street names shown on it. One from Yellow Pages or your Thomson local directory may be suitable. If the school is in a rural area you can use the map of a nearby built-up shopping area that pupils are familiar with. Choose a starting point on the map. It can be the school or some other place that everybody knows.

Write out a list of six finishing points for each pair of pupils. To begin with it is probably better to have finishing points that are fairly close to the starting point and only need simple directions.

Leading the activity
Make sure that the pupils understand the instructions in the pupil's book. Then let them go ahead with the activity.

We often use landmarks like pubs and traffic lights when giving directions; these will not be shown on the map, so this activity forces pupils to use the 'first on the left, second on the right' approach. You could make a teaching point about these differing ways of giving directions.

If pupils are confident about direction-giving you can make the starting and finishing points more challenging.

Page 12 **Raffle**

This gives practice in working out multiples of 5p and in converting between numbers written out in words and numbers written out in figures.

1 The tickets cost 20p.

2 They cost 35p.

3 Ken can buy 6 tickets.

4 They will cost Frances 50p.

5 Pam can get 20 tickets.

6 They sell 200 tickets.

7 37

8 14

9 90

Checking and supporting

Difficulties with elementary number work of this kind may be deep-rooted and are likely to need careful and repeated work over time if they are to be put right.

If, in questions **1** to **5**, pupils have difficulty with multiples of 5p, don't assume that attention to the five times table or setting out of written working are all that is needed: these approaches have probably been tried with them many times before and evidently have not worked. Instead, first check whether pupils are properly familiar with the coinage; devise activities with real coins, in which they have to be sure of their values and the ways they can be exchanged (for example, that a 20p coin can be exchanged for four 5p coins). This serves as a useful reminder, by the way, that change giving is not just about counting on or subtraction; it involves multiplication and division ideas as well, and these need to be brought out in discussion during practice with money.

Success with question **6** suggests a fair degree of confidence in dealing with money. Questions **7** to **9** should help you identify two kinds of difficulty – the confusion between 14 and 40 and thinking of 307 as thirty-seven. The first problem is sometimes sorted out straight away by pointing out to pupils that 14 and 40 sound very similar and that they must listen very carefully to distinguish between them. The second may indicate a fundamental misunderstanding of place value and, if so, you will need to work carefully and repeatedly over time with the pupil to rectify the problems.

Extra practice

This can take the form of various count-round games, with each different type done on a *separate* occasion (see page 7 for a general description of count-round games). To reinforce the whole numbers between 1 and 100 start at, say, 38 and get pupils to count up in ones. When they are confident get them to count down in ones. To reinforce the multiples of 5p, get them to count up '5p, 10p, 15p, ...' and then when they are confident to count down.

Questions **7** to **9** can be supported with several speaking, listening and writing activities. Check that pupils can say the names of individual digits out loud; give practice if necessary. Then give them practice in reading complete numbers out loud ('forty-seven', 'two hundred and sixty-two'), including reading out numbers from a calculator display.

For another practice activity make cards containing numbers written in figures: pupils A and B sit back to back; A has one of the cards and reads out each number out in words and B writes it down again in figures; A and B then check by comparing the numbers on the card with those that B wrote down. (Eavesdrop to check that A is reading out complete numbers, not separate digits.)

Pupils can also work in pairs to practice putting numbers in order. One pupil says a few numbers between 1 and 100 in any order. The other has to write them down and then put them in the right order.

Various pieces of software reinforce awareness of the 1 to 100 number line (see planner table on pages 20–21).

Page 13 | ## 5s with hexagons Allow at least half an hour

'They enjoyed it, they loved it: they were quite eager to go and try and better themselves.'

This game provides practice in mentally finding numbers that add up to five. A certain amount of strategic skill is needed to put the last few hexagons in place, but trialling showed that pupils enjoyed the challenge. The value of work like this is that pupils concentrate on the game and the mental arithmetic comes naturally. As the scoring implies, a board that is not quite complete may be a significant achievement for some pupils.

The game **10s with triangles** (page 30) has exactly the same structure as this one, except that there pairs of numbers have to add up to ten.

Before you start

You need worksheets **A1–1** and **A1–2**. If you reproduce several sets of the hexagons drawn on **A1–1** it is a good idea to print each set on a different coloured card: the hexagons are difficult to sort and the game will be difficult, if not impossible, with a mixed set. Decide whether you want to cut out the hexagons in advance or whether you want the pupils to do it.

Page 14 Compass directions

A useful supplement for pupils using the Green series or the many others who have difficulty with this topic; links with *Book G2* p.57 **Review: directions.**

The main problem with compass directions is that they work relative to some particular point on the earth's surface. Yet some pupils tend to think of north as the name of a *place* to go towards (this confusion is reinforced by our use of phrases like 'the north' to mean an area of the country).

We have done three things in this chapter to try to help the situation. First we reinforce the idea of north as a *direction*, not a place, by showing a series of parallel lines all marked north. Secondly the compass rose, rather than appearing once in a fixed place on the map, is turned into a moveable compass pointer on a small square of clear acetate; the pupil carries around this tangible reminder of the compass directions and put it down on the place from which directions are being considered. Thirdly we spell out the compass direction words in full rather than give them in their rather abstract abbreviated form.

The chapter could play a part in joint work with the geography department.

Classroom organisation

Pupils can work alone for most of the chapter but need to work in pairs for the challenge on worksheet **A1– 4**.

Before you start

You need a compass pointer for each pupil: photocopy worksheet **A1–3** on to acetate; each acetate sheet gives nine compass pointers. These are cheap enough to become part of each pupil's personal 'school equipment kit' if you wish. Each pupil also needs worksheets **A1–4** and **A1–5**. You may need slide **A1–OHP2**.

A Pigeon racing

A confusing variety of language is used when talking about compass directions (what direction is A from B ? what direction do you have to go from C to get to D? E is to the north of F, and so on). This work incorporates that variety yet the pigeon racing context helps pupils make sense of how the direction language has to be used.

Introducing the topic

If you want to introduce the topic to the whole class or a large group within the class, you can use slide **A1–OHP2** to show how the compass pointer is used and to lead a question-and-answer session.

A1 Manchester is west from Sheffield.

A2 They fly north from Stoke-on-Trent.

A3 They fly south-west from Leeds.

A4 They fly east from Liverpool.

A5 They fly north from Coventry.

A6 They fly east from Stoke-on-Trent.

 A7 Nottingham is to the **south** of York.

A8 Leeds is to the **west** of Hull.
If you go further west you get to **Bradford**.
Derby is to the **south-west** of Hull.

A9 Nottingham is to the north of **Leicester**.
Sheffield is to the south of **Leeds**.

A10 Leicester is **north-east** of Coventry.
Nottingham is **south-west** of Lincoln.
Liverpool is **west** of Manchester and **north-west** of Stoke-on-Trent.

A11 Derby is north of **Coventry**.
Derby is **north-west** of Leicester.
To fly from Lincoln to Leeds a bird would have to go **north-west**.
Nottingham is to the **south-east** of Manchester.
Birmingham is to the south-west of Nottingham.

A12 Tanya and her pigeons live in **Sheffield**.

T

Checking and supporting

It is worth taking time to go over these questions with pupils to make sure they are thinking and not just following a reflex. When only one town is mentioned in a question and pupils have to fill another town in a blank, they tend to put the centre of the compass pointer on the town that is given, rather than think about the right thing to do. Although we have put some heavy hints about this in questions **A9** and **A10** on worksheet **A1–4**, you should check at this point. You could ask questions of the same type orally later. In some of the later questions cities line up with the compass directions only roughly. Introduce phrases like 'roughly south-east' if you think it is necessary.

Follow up work

Pupils can work with compass directions on 'real' maps, using the compass pointer if necessary.

Page 16 **B At the funfair**

A1–5 ▶

He came to the entrance gate and walked **west** to the car park.

Then he walked **north** and then **east** to the Octopus.

Then he went **north** and rode on the Cup and saucers.

Mike went **north-west** towards the cafe, where he had some pizza and coke.

Then he went **north** to ride on the Rapids and **east** for a ride on the Big wheel.

By now he was feeling sick and decided to head for the toilets.

He walked **east** past the railway and then **south.**

After that Mike decided to take things easy and watch the boats on the lake.

He went **south** from the toilets and then **west** to the boating lake.

He felt much better. So he headed **south-west** to the car park and walked **east** towards the entrance gate.

Challenge

The pupils' descriptions of their own routes

Checking and supporting

Look to see whether pupils are doing this section without the compass pointer. If they are it suggests that they are remembering the compass directions and understand that they are always relative to some point on the map. But don't discourage those who still want to use the pointer.

In the open-ended challenge pupils can make their route for the day out as difficult as their confidence and competence allow. You could encourage a discussion of how good each route was (judged by the pupils' own standards).

Page 18 # Newsagent

This gives practice in multiplication and addition of small amounts of money.

▶ 1   (a) Jason pays 20p.
   (b) No, he will not have any money left.

2   Sally will have 1p left.

3   (a) Any combination costing 20p or less
   (b) The change from 20p for the pupil's choice

4   The pupil's choice costing 20p

5   The pupil's choice for 50p or less

Checking and supporting

You can use this page for one-to-one discussion with the pupil to identify any difficulties. Any that you find should be tackled with the aid of real coins, rather than by focusing on pure arithmetic.

Extra practice

You can turn the story into a competitive game for teacher and pupil or two pupils: one says something like 'Two shrimps and a fried egg' quickly and the other has to say the total cost.

If you find that pupils lack confidence with the coinage, now is the time to provide extra help. For example, put pupils in pairs with some coins: one has to state an amount of money less than £1 and the other has to make it.

Page 19 # Toast and tallies

A useful supplement for pupils following the Green series. The tallying links with *Book G1* p.39 **Dice** and p.48 **Detective dice**, though the context there is an experiment, rather than a survey.

The chapter emphasises that surveys should be done for a purpose and in an efficient and unbiased way.

A Things people prefer

The pupil's book assumes the ability to read from a tally chart and fill one in. Some pupils will need extra help with this. We always use the convention of grouping tallies in fives with the first four vertical and a diagonal stroke completing the five. Remember that a tally chart is sometimes a good way to count and in other circumstances a very inefficient one. It is useful when the different sorts of things that you will be counting come at you in a random way as, for instance, when you go out on a survey. But when items to be counted are presented together, for example on a printed page, it is often better just to count those of a certain type and write down the total, then do the same for those of another type and so on.

A1 They could ask 'What type of jam, if any, do you prefer?'

A2 (a) 12 pupils (b) 29 pupils (c) 41 pupils

A3 (a) 6 pupils (b) 29 pupils (c) 35 pupils

A4 Thick toast with margarine should sell well, but it might be sensible to give a wider choice.

Page 20 A5 They get different results because Paul leads people to choose chocolate spread and puts them off marmalade.

A6 Saiqa's survey is more useful, because it is not biased.

Discussing the answers

Take the opportunity to make the point that the aim of a survey is to get accurate information. Discuss the ways we use the words 'bias' and 'biased'.

B Recording results

This provides practice at tallying within the confines of the classroom.

Page 21 ## C Surveys that went wrong

This section points to some common pitfalls (and remedies) in carrying out surveys. Most teachers would agree that the cartoons are not too much of an exaggeration. If problems arise in later survey work you can bring pupils back to these pages and draw their attention to these situations.

Page 22 ## D Your own survey

Suitable topics for pupils' own surveys include favourite sports, chocolate bars, crisp flavours, fizzy drinks, TV channels, clothes and features of cars in the school car park such as their year of registration letter, colour, make and number of doors. It is worth making sure that the topic for a survey is not one that pupils have done before.

Page 23 ## E Toast again

E1 (a) They sold 34 slices.   (b) They sold 75 slices.
(c) They sold 46 slices.

E2 (a) The machine probably broke down on Wednesday.
(b) They sold more toast that day, probably because people came for toast instead of snacks from the machine.

E3

Day	Number of slices sold	Profit(p)	Profit (£)
Mon	22	154p	£1·54
Tue	34	238p	£2·38
Wed	75	525p	£5·25
Thu	51	357p	£3·57
Fri	46	322p	£3·22
Total		1596p	£15·96

E4 They can send £15·96 to the charity.

Checking and supporting

Question **E3** may reveal problems about knowing when and how to multiply on a calculator. Pupils also need to convert a calculator result in pence into one in pounds. If necessary, ask further questions of this type while discussing the section.

Page 24 ## Pinball wizard

This involves the addition of simple one- and two-digit numbers.

Before you start

Each pupil needs worksheet **A1–6**.

> **A1–6**

1 Kate has scored 50 points.

2 Joe has scored 48 points.

3 The pupil's own way of scoring 26

4 The pupil's own way of scoring 26

5 The pupil's own turns at pinball

Checking and supporting

Some pupils may be able to do these questions mentally, but encourage those who cannot to show working in a way that they find helpful.

Page 25 ## Symmetrical letters and masks

Links with *Book G1* p.22 **Review: reflection** and *Book G2* p.39 **Review: reflection.**

The work draws attention to the way symmetrical shapes are generated and offers rich opportunities for links with art. In this chapter there is only ever a single vertical line of symmetry. Patterns with a non-vertical line of symmetry and with more than one line of symmetry are explored in *Book A2* page 29 **Patterns by folding and cutting.**

Classroom organisation

This chapter makes an ideal whole class activity and, although it takes a long time, the teachers who trialled it were happy to do it as one continuous piece of work stretching over several lessons.

Before you start

Each pupil needs four pieces of tracing paper (about 5 cm square), sticky tape, and felt tips or crayons and elastic, worksheets **A1–7**, **A1–8** and **A1–9**.

A1–8 and **A1–9** should be reproduced on white card; alternatively reproduce them on paper and after pupils have drawn and coloured their masks they can glue the worksheets on to cornflake packet cardboard before cutting the masks out.

A Making letters

This introduces the idea that the half-shape is systematically transferred to the other side to make the symmetrical letter.

 A1–7

A1 The result should be the word WAVY.

A2 The result should be the word MOUTH.

Page 26

B Making a symmetrical mask · Allow at least one hour

A1–8

Pupils enjoy doing this activity and its counterpart in section D; their skill in observing one side of the mask and drawing the other side to correspond seems to improve as a result of the work. When we tried this out, pupils were happy to have their masks made into wall displays: it was a source of pride for them and other groups who saw the displays wanted to do the masks too. Don't miss these sections out. The time they take is worth it.

REFLECTION
SYMMETRY

'One or two found some difficulty and needed extra help with completing the second half of the mask, but learnt more about symmetry, especially when colouring in the first mask. They then set about designing their own correctly with great gusto!'

Checking and supporting

Even though the dots provide a structure for the work, difficulties may arise with the dots that are well away from the centre line. One boy with severe learning difficulties was determined to produce a mask. His teacher encouraged him to check his work by using tracing paper with a dotted line on, as he had done with the letters on worksheet **A1–7**. This helped him a lot, though he was keen to show his independence by managing without it whenever he could.

C Masks from around the world

Teacher-led discussion

Rather than have pupils work independently, merely writing short answers into their exercise books, it is much better to run this section as a class discussion. If pupils think a mask isn't symmetrical, invite them to say what features differ from side to side. While some of the masks have subtle disparities, in one case they are stark though far from obvious at first glance. Encourage the use of language to describe shapes, sizes and positions.

If they say (for example) the left eye in (h) is winking, ask them whether they mean left 'as we see it' or left 'from the mask's point of view' (a follow up from the chapter **Left and right**).

Page 27   ▶   **C1** (a) Symmetrical
       (b) Not symmetrical
       (c) Not symmetrical, because the two halves
           of the mask are different colours.
Page 28   (d) Symmetrical
       (e) Not symmetrical
       (f) Symmetrical
Page 29   (g) Not symmetrical
       (h) Not symmetrical

D Making your own mask

A1–9   With luck, pupils will have gained artistic inspiration from the previous section, which will help them as they now design their own mask.

Page 30   # 10s with triangles

The structure of this game is exactly the same as in **5s with hexagons** (page 13), so if pupils have played that game there should be no difficulty in understanding the rules for this one. You may need to explain the use of underlining to distinguish between 6 and 9.

Before you start

You need worksheets **A1–10** and **A1–11**. If you reproduce several sets of the triangles drawn on **A1–10** it is a good idea to print each set on a different coloured card: the triangles are difficult to sort and the game will be difficult, if not impossible, with a mixed set. Decide whether you want to cut out the triangles in advance or whether you want the pupils to do it.

Page 31 **Chocolate boxes**

This exercise in adding small amounts of money also requires a certain amount of organisational skill.

Before you start

Each pupil needs one copy of worksheet **A1–12**. You may also need copies of worksheet **A1–13** for further challenges.

A1–12 ▶

1 The pupil's box for Zara and its price

2 The pupil's own box and price

3 The cheapest selection should total 53p.

4 The most expensive selection should total 80p.

Checking and supporting

Questions **3** and **4** require a systematic approach in identifying the cheapest and most expensive chocolates. Encourage pupils to describe their own methods for sorting this out.

Extra practice

Worksheet **A1–13** is for you to make up some further challenges such as:
   'Can you put eight chocolates that cost 60p in a box?'
   'Can you put eight chocolates all the same in a box so that it costs 40p?'
   'Can you use just two kinds of chocolates to get a total of…'
   …and so on.

Page 32 **Car boot sale**

Links with *Book G1* p.14 **Money** and p.20 **Money games.**

The chapter provides practice in finding the total cost of purchases and giving change, with the amounts restricted to multiples of 5p for the smaller amounts and to multiples of 50p for the larger amounts.

Before you start

You will need some coins for practice and sorting out difficulties. Real coins are always preferable to plastic ones, so for practical purposes it may be better to have only a small group at a time working on sections A and B (and possibly also C); this will also allow you to check that each pupil is competent with all the basic techniques that are involved. It may be better not to do the whole chapter in one go.

A Angie's stall

Introducing the topic

Potential problems with adding and multiplying small amounts of money should have been identified in **Newsagent**, questions **E3** and **E4** of **Toast and tallies**, and **Chocolate boxes**. You can remind pupils of those chapters while introducing this chapter if you wish. It is also worth checking now that no one missed them through absence. If you needed to give a pupil extra support with those chapters now is the time to check that it was effective.

It may be a good idea to do a few questions in the style of **A2** orally before pupils start work on their own, to get them used to having to search in the photo for prices.

▶ **A1** (a) 60p   (b) 60p

A2 (a) 40p   (b) 40p   (c) 30p   (d) £1   (e) 90p
    (f) £1·50   (g) 70p   (h) 75p   (i) £1·80

A3

4 mugs cost	£1·00
4 dishes cost	£0·60
4 plates cost	£2·00
Total cost	£3·60

A4

(a)

2 comics cost	£0·20
3 dishes cost	£0·45
2 toy cars cost	£0·60
Total cost	£1·25

(b)

5 egg cups cost	£0·50
1 plant pot holder costs	£0·75
2 posters cost	£0·90
Total cost	£2·15

Checking and supporting

If pupils encounter difficulties here, initial support work using 5p and 10p coins is likely to be more successful than using the full range of coins.

Play count-round games going up in 5p or 10p steps (pupils have to remember to say the 'p' each time).

For each sum, you can also help by encouraging pupils to set out the coins needed for each of the objects individually, before they count up the total.

Questions **A3** and **A4** may reveal a number of difficulties including unfamiliarity with the idea of adding more than two numbers together; pupils may of course write out their bills in pence.

Page 33 **B Giving change on Angie's stall**

The change giving is not done by formal subtraction here but by 'adding-on'. Perhaps you use mental subtraction when dealing with change yourself, but adding-on is the method most used by shop staff (those who don't have tills that work out the change for them). The sequence of illustrations in section B provides a model for the adding-on process: the basic idea is that the customer hands the stall keeper some money, then the stall keeper *hands back the same total value* in the form of the object sold plus the counted-on change. If you have never done this yourself try practising with a colleague first as it may not feel very natural. Then set up practice situations in the classroom where two pupils (or you and one pupil) are the buyer and the seller.

▶ **B1** and **B2** Observation of the pupil's counting on

B3 (a) 80p   (b) 20p

B4 35p

Page 34 **C Ted's stall**

Here the prices are nearly always multiples of 50p.

▶ **C1** (a) £4   (b) £5·75   (c) £5   (d) £6

C2 Ajit spent the most money.

C3 (a) £3   (b) £2

C4 50p

C5 £1·50

Page 35 **C6** (a) Jigsaw puzzle   (b) 75p

C7 (a) Typewriter   (b) £8

C8 £5

C9 (a) £2   (b) No

C10 £2

C11 The pupil's own answers

Page 36 **Cubes in a mirror** Allow at least 20 minutes

This activity offers some very informal and low-key experience of the ideas of a mirror image and reflection symmetry in three dimensions. The concept of a plane of symmetry is not introduced at this stage.

Classroom organisation

Pupils need to work in pairs. This doesn't need to be done by the whole class together. It makes a good half-lesson 'filler' activity, but you will need to allow time to look at the models pupils make and discuss them with them.

Before you start

Each pair of pupils needs about 10 multilink cubes. You need at least one plastic mirror in case pupils ask for it.

Page 37 **10s on a grid**

Links with 'Number noughts and crosses' in *Resource pack B* card 14 **Noughts and...** , which is, however, harder because pupils have to make a total of 15.

The game **10s with triangles** on page 30 was about finding pairs of numbers that add up to 10; now larger groups that add to 10 are required. The game requires a fair amount of strategy.

Before you start

You need a 1–6 dice and a copy of worksheet **A1–14** for each pair of pupils. Make sure each pair has access to pens of two different colours.

 The question about Jatinder is best approached by discussion, with his grid drawn on the blackboard.

1	1	2	
2		3	1
2	1	↖2	
	4		

—He should put his 5 here.

Page 38 **Map grids**

A useful supplement for pupils following the Green series

This deals with the convention of using coordinates (like 'B4') to denote a *square* on a map (rather than a point).

Classroom organisation

The chapter is designed to be done by pupils working in pairs.

Before you start

For each pair of pupils doing the game 'Treasure' you need two six-sided dice, one labelled 1–6 in the ordinary way, the other labelled A to F (write the letters on an adhesive address label, cut them out and stick them on to a standard dice, or write directly on to a blank dice), and the treasure tokens made from worksheet **A1–15** (decide whether to cut them out in advance or to let the pupils do it). If you reproduce several sets of treasure tokens it is a good idea to have each set on different coloured card, to prevent sets from being mixed up. You may need slide **A1–OHP3**. For extra practice after section B you will need a map with a street index.

A Treasure

This game provides an appealing introduction to the square numbering convention and an incentive to become confident in using it. The rules have been kept to a minimum, so one or two things may need to be sorted out as the game proceeds (for example, is the free pardon to count as a piece of treasure for the purpose of swapping?).

Checking and supporting

Eavesdrop to check that pupils *are* referring to 'B4' and not '4B'.

Page 40 ## B Using a street index

Using a map with an index is an important skill, which can add enormously to people's confidence and independence when they are in a town or city that they do not know well.

Introducing the topic

You can use slide **A1–OHP3** for a teacher-led session. Pupils can come out to the projector to point to streets that they have found.

Checking and supporting

For many pupils the most daunting thing about this work is that the names of the streets are unfamiliar. Encourage them: explain that if you were in a strange town they would be unfamiliar to you too. Efficient use of an index depends on good knowledge of the alphabet. Although this is less critical with a short list of streets like this one, if you detect a problem it is worth taking action, either as part of your own contribution to special needs or by consulting colleagues in the English department.

Extra practice

You can use this map for other activities, such as giving and following directions as in section D of **Left and right**. Slide **A1–OHP3** can be used for this work too: you can 'orientate' the slide on the projector to help pupils see whether they have correctly identified a left or right turn. This is perhaps best done on a different occasion from the map index work.

Extension

If pupils have done the activity confidently they can, if you wish, go on to use a commercially produced map with a street index. It's a big jump, though, and will require care: sorting out the squares on the bigger map will be harder, and the index will be longer. The conventional abbreviations on street maps can be off-putting ('Ct', 'Ln', the two occurrences of 'St' in 'St Mary's St') and are worth taking some time over. Street plans for larger cities often come in book form and if you use one you will have to explain how the page number is included in every street reference.

Page 42 # Early starters

This chapter on telling the time is designed to allow the early diagnosis of problems that could form an insuperable barrier in more difficult work. It should allow you to check that the pupil has some understanding of the relationship between a time written in numbers, how it looks on a clock face and how it looks written out in words. The ability to put times in order is also checked. The times are all whole hours, halves and quarters. Restricting the events to the period between midnight and noon means that a.m. and p.m. don't enter in as additional complications at this stage. Telling the time is picked up again in *Book A2* page 24 **Clock watching** (see page 61 of this guide).

Classroom organisation

Because of its diagnostic purpose, it is better if this chapter is done by pupils working on their own.

Before you start

Each pupil needs the cards cut out from worksheets **A1–16** and **A1–17**.

Checking and supporting

Although the pupil's book asks for the times to be copied out from the cards arranged on the table to give you a permanent record to check, it is better if you are present to watch the activity being done.

Even the more confident pupils may need to be helped with linking 'quarter to' with the '45' in times written out in figures.

Less confident pupils may do better to use just the 'o'clock' and 'half past ' cards to start with, leaving 'quarter to' and 'quarter past' until later.

In addition, preliminary individual work with a clock can be helpful (an old real clock is a good deal cheaper – and less primary-schoolish – than the geared token clocks that educational suppliers sell). Turn the hands and talk through the times on the hour from 12 o'clock round to 12 o'clock again; then go through again in order, saying the half hours as well. During this work you can establish the meaning of the word clockwise.

A pupil who finds it hard to distinguish between the hour hand and the minute hand may be helped by using a token clock which only has an hour hand on it. (You can explain that long ago clocks only had an hour hand and marks for the hours; when people wanted to tell the time more accurately they made clocks with another, longer hand, and added marks around the clock for the minutes.) Show how the small hour hand gradually moves round clockwise.

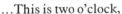

…This is two o'clock,   …this is half past two   …and this is three o'clock.

If you have diagnosed difficulties with time and seem to have overcome them by providing extra help, you will need to come back to the topic fairly soon, as these ideas are easily forgotten if not practised.

Wherever possible use real time passing, not only to help pupils read a clock but also to improve their 'feel' for time – for when it is about three o'clock in the afternoon, for example.

Extra practice

Consider a count-round game based on the quarter hours: 'Two o'clock, quarter past two, half past two, quarter to three, ...' (see page 7 for a general comment on count-round games).

Talk about somebody's day (the pupils' own, a friend's, a relative's, a famous person's). Discuss what they do and the times that they do it. Ask pupils to write down the events and times in order.

Page 44 # Review: pages 4 to 12

A Left and right

▶ **A1** The other runner is behind Sonia's left arm.

A2 You get to the park.

A3 One possible route is:

Turn left out of the school gate.
Take the first right.
Then the first right again.
Take the first left.
You get to a T-junction and the post office is straight ahead across the road.

Extra practice
In question **A2** you can ask for directions between other pairs of places.

B Money practice

▶ **B1** (a) 6p   (b) 10p   (c) 15p   (d) 26p

Page 45 # Review: pages 13 to 23

Before you start
Each pupil needs worksheet **A1–18** and a compass pointer.

A Puzzle it out

A1–18 ▶

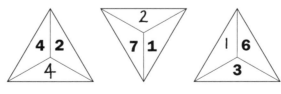

Two ten triples of the pupil's own

1	7	8
5	3	8
6	10	16

6	4	10
7	3	10
13	7	20

9	2	11
5	2	7
14	4	18

7	4	11
1	6	7
8	10	18

B Compass directions

B1 (a) They fly north.
(b) They fly east.
(c) They fly north-east.

C Surveys

C1 He has put a 5 instead of a 6 for the number of people who preferred ham.

C2 Cheese is the most popular.

C3 Salad is the least popular.

C4 Baljit asked 40 people.

Page 46 # Review: pages 14 to 29

Before you start

Each pupil needs worksheet **A1–19**. Pupils may ask for a compass pointer.

A Symmetrical shapes

The drawings are quite demanding, so you should be ready to give support.

   The pupil's drawings on the worksheet

B Compass directions

B1 (a) London is **north** of Brighton.
(b) Bristol is **north-east** of Plymouth.
(c) Portsmouth is **south-east** of Southampton and west of **Brighton**.

C Money practice

C1 You can buy a pencil and rubber for 17p.

C2 There are various combinations.

C3 They will cost 86p.

C4 The pupil's choice of coins

Page 47   **Review:** pages 30 to 36

Before you start
Each pupil needs worksheets **A1–20** and **A1–21**, scissors and glue.

A Puzzle it out

Links with *Resource pack A* card 20 **Arithmogons**.

A1–20

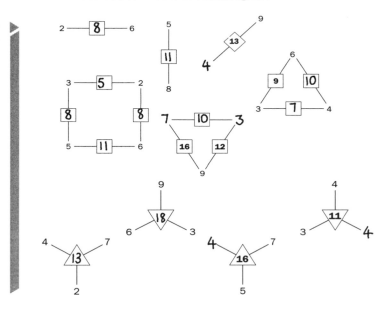

B Number practice

Links with *Resource pack A* card 22 **Stamps**.

A1–21 ▶ The pupil's arrangement of stamps

C Giving change

C1 She gets 25p change.

C2 You get 13p change.

C3 He gets 35p change.

C4 You get £3·50 change.

C5 You get £2·50 change.

D Cubes in a mirror

▶ (a) and (c) would look the same in the mirror.

Page 48 **Review:** **pages 37 to 43**

Before you start

Each pupil needs worksheet **A1–22**.

A Puzzle it out

A1–22 ▶

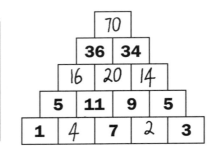
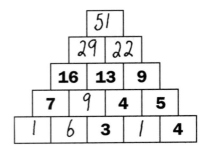

B A grid code

▶ The message is 'This is secret.'

C Time

▶ **C1** (a) Four o'clock   4:00
(b) Half past nine   9:30
(c) Quarter to one   12:45
(d) Half past six   6:30
(e) Quarter past eleven   11:15
(f) Ten o'clock   10:00
(g) Quarter to nine   8:45
(h) Quarter past nine   9:15

Book A2

This book aims to maintain the enjoyment that we hope pupils have derived from *Book A1*. At the same time we offer opportunities for pupils to gain confidence in further technical skills. For example, the number work, which in *Book A1* was broadly limited to comparison, addition, subtraction and a limited set of multiplications, now moves on to include a greater emphasis on multiplication and some simple but thorough work on halving.

Once again, many of the chapters are designed to be teacher led.

Mathematical themes in this book

Patterns on tiles and **Box curves** allow you to check whether pupils are familiar with a ruler and provide an incentive for them to do some accurate technical drawing. **Patterns by folding and cutting** develops ideas of symmetry beyond those met in *Book A1*. **Right-angles** depends for its effectiveness on teacher-led discussion and begins a strand of work, continued in *Book A3*, that helps pupils appreciate important geometrical features in the world around them.

Getting it taped and **Clock watching** continue a carefully developed strand of work on time, which began with the diagnostic chapter **Early starters** in *Book A1*. Informal ideas of metric weights and how heavy they feel is developed in **Weighing it up**.

Practice in comparing lengths of time and amounts of money is incorporated into the data sorting activity **Cookery cards**.

Multiplication is developed further in **Grouping and multiplication**, with follow-up practice provided in **Multiplication bingo** and other activities described in this teacher's guide. The table on page 8 of this guide shows the multiplication facts that we expect for *Book A2*.

Going halves is about halving amounts of money and provides further practice with coins. Halves, halving and quarters have already appeared in the book, for example in **Patterns on tiles**, the time chapters, **Right-angles** (page 16 where the right-angle is seen as a quarter circle) and **Patterns by folding and cutting**; so you can with benefit keep referring to them in teacher-led revision.

Planner table for Book A2 (see p.12)

Page	Chapter	Worksheets (see pp.13–15)	Links with later work in Amber
4	**Patterns on tiles** Measurement and accurate drawing	A2–1 A2–2	A2 p.43 **Box curves**
6	**Top secret message** Code that provides arithmetic practice		
7	**Getting it taped** Using 60 minutes in an hour	A2–3 A2–4	A2 p.24 **Clock watching**
11	**Grouping and multiplication** Reinforcement of multiplication facts	A2–5 A2–6 A2–7	A2 p.40 **Multiplication bingo**
15	**Right-angles** Finding right-angles and why they are useful	A2–8 A2–9	A3 p.12 **Horizontal** A3 p.29 **Vertical**
22	**Cookery cards** Sorting activity based on choices of meals	A2–10 A2–11 A2–12	A3 p.8 **Gardens**
24	**Clock watching** Elementary work on telling the time	A2–13 A2–14 A2–OHP1	A3 p.20 **a.m. and p.m.**
28	**Target 30** Game giving practice in mental addition		A3 p.34 **Honeycombs**
29	**Patterns by folding and cutting** Patterns that have a line of symmetry at an angle or several lines of symmetry	A2–15 A2–16 A2–17 A2–18	
35	**Going halves** Halving amounts of money	A2–19 A2–20	A3 p.11 **Halving recipes** A3 p.24 **Cafe**
40	**Multiplication bingo** Game to practice mental multiplication	A2–21	A3 p.24 **Cafe**
41	**Weighing it up** Getting a feel for metric weights		A3 p.28 **Make a kilogram** A3 p.41 **Kitchen scales**
43	**Box curves** Using accurate measurement to produce attractive patterns	A2–22	A3 p.4 **Rulers**
44	**Review: Book A1 and pages 4 to 10**	A2–23 A2–24	
45	**Review: Book A1 and pages 6 to 21**	A2–25	
46	**Review: Book A1 and pages 11 to 27**		
47	**Review: pages 15 to 34**	A2–26	
48	**Review: pages 24 to 42** Multiplication cards (see pp.70–71 of this guide)	A2–27 A2–28 A2–29 A2–30	

Links with work in Green and Resource packs	Recommended software	National references		
		England and Wales	**Northern Ireland**	**Scotland**
G4 p.36 **Square pattern**		AT3 level 2	ATS level 3	Measure and estimate level B
G2 p.40 **Button pressing**		AT2 level 3	ATN level 2	Add and subtract level B Multiply and divide level B
		AT3 level 3	ATM level 2	Time
		AT2 level 3	ATN level 3	Multiply and divide level B
G1 p.13 **Review: angle**		AT3 level 2	ATS level 3	Angle level B
		AT4 level 2	ATD level 2	Organise level A
G1 p.32 **Time** G2 p.19 **Time** **Time refreshers 1 and 2** in Worksheets for the G series		AT3 level 3	ATM level 3	Time level B
G1 p.56 **The keyboard game** Resource pack B card 24 **Stepping stones**	**Trains** in Straker 6 is simple with a primary feel. **Make 37** in Straker 5 is motivating and needs some strategy.	AT2 level 3	ATN level 2	Add and subtract level B
Resource pack B card 23 **Symmetry**		AT3 level 4	ATS level 3	Symmetry levels B, D
G1 p.14 **Money**		AT2 level 3	ATN level 3	Money level C Fractions, percentages and ratio level B
		AT2 level 3	ATN level 3	Multiply and divide level B
G2 p.12 **How heavy?**		AT3 level 2	ATM level 3	Measure and estimate level B
		AT3 level 2	ATM level 3	Measure and estimate level B

Resource pack B card 11
Add ups

Patterns on tiles Allow about one and a half to three hours.

Links with *Book G4* p.36 **Square pattern**, which is, however, harder, requiring division on a calculator, interpretation of the calculator result and measurement to the nearest millimetre.

This activity gives practice in measuring and assumes some previous experience. Pupils see that by starting with a simple element (a square) and following simple instructions they can produce an impressive pattern. Measurements are made horizontally, vertically and diagonally. Even though all the lengths are whole centimetres the activity provides an incentive to measure accurately, since even a very small error will distort the pattern produced.

Classroom organisation

This is most effective as a group or whole-class activity, as it can contribute to a sense of shared achievement, especially if you take the opportunity to make a classroom display of the finished work. It will also be easier for you to watch for pupils who are uncertain what to do or who are not measuring accurately.

Before you start

Each pupil needs one copy of worksheets **A2–1** and **A2–2**.

Teacher-led discussion

After pupils have done patterns **2** and **3** you can talk about the effects of joining several of these designs together. Indeed your classroom display can bring out these effects. You can also explain that getting tiles to match up is another reason for producing them accurately.

Checking and supporting

Pupils may still make common errors when using a ruler – not recognising the centimetre unit or aligning the end of the ruler or the 1 cm mark with the end of the line. Consider demonstrating on an overhead projector with an appropriate acetate ruler from **A3–OHP1**. Some pupils will spot their mistakes from the distorting effect they have on their designs and may be able to put them right themselves.

The diagrams in the pupil's book suggest making a perpendicular mark to indicate a position that has been measured off.

Those who are satisfied with this kind of mark need an explanation of why we have to mark accurately.

We put the perpendicular mark outside the tile to avoid this error, which came up during trialling:

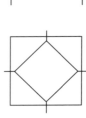

Pattern **4** allows pupils to think up their own ways of generating new designs. Some may be short of ideas, in which case you could suggest that they begin with a 3 by 3 or 4 by 4 grid of the kind used in pattern **3**. Be prepared, too, for pupils who quickly and enthusiastically produce designs of their own, but which are not generated by formal geometrical processes like those used so far.

Page 6 # Top secret message

Links with *Book G2* p.40 **Button pressing**, which concentrates on matching arithmetic operations to real-life situations.

This activity involves the recognition of addition, subtraction and multiplication words and symbols as well as offering practice in mental calculation. The need to finish with a coherent message motivates pupils to identify and correct their own errors.

Classroom organisation

This is best done with pupils working in pairs so that they can make up their own coded messages and try them on their partner.

26 → S	18 → A	8 → Y	20 → T
23 → M	20 → T	22 → O	24 → E
16 → I		12 → U	18 → A
13 → L		15 → R	25 → C
24 → E			7 → H
			24 → E
			15 → R

Checking and supporting

Some things, like the word 'tripled' and the fact that 'five less than twenty' is not 5 – 20, may be unfamiliar and, if so, will need to be worked on. Pupils will need to hear any new words ('Let's practise doing some tripling.'), and should have practice in saying them. When you ask the pupils to produce their own coded messages you could issue a checklist of words and phrases that have to be used at least once, for example '… less than …' '… take away …' '… more than …' 'double …' '… minus …' '… tripled'.

   Alternatively you could challenge pupils to include in their messages as many different words and phrases for calculations as they can.

   If the activity reveals that a pupil has difficulty with particular number bonds or other elements of mental arithmetic you should make a note of them so that you can do follow-up work later.

Page 7 **Getting it taped**

This chapter is part of a careful progression of work on time that begins with **Early starters** in *Book A1* and continues with **Clock watching** in the present book, then **a.m. and p.m.** and **24-hour times** in *Book A3*. The chapter aims to reinforce the fact that 60 minutes make one hour and to provide practice in combining lengths of time (which are restricted to multiples of five minutes). It also uses the ideas of a quarter, a half and three-quarters of an hour together with their equivalents in minutes.

Classroom organisation

The work can be done individually.

Before you start

Pupils will need the programme cards made from worksheet **A2–3** and the sports cards made from worksheet **A2–4**; in both cases it will help to have cut the cards out in advance.

A Video time

> **A1** These pairs make 1 hour of TV:
>
> Phone-in and Local News
> Comedy Spot and Serial
> News and Pop-slot
> Chat show and Cartoon
> Film and Weather
>
> **A2** The programme lasts 20 minutes.

Page 8   **A3** They fit exactly on the clock face.

Page 9   **A4** and **A5**

There are many ways of making 3 separate hours of sport, for example:

Rugby	45 minutes	Skiing	25 minutes
Weight lifting	15 minutes	Half time results	5 minutes
		Gymnastics	20 minutes
Volleyball	15 minutes	Swimming	10 minutes
Show jumping	15 minutes		
Bowls	15 minutes		
Basketball	10 minutes		
Table tennis	5 minutes		

Fifteen minutes of sport will be left.

A6 (a) There are 30 minutes in half an hour.

(b) Here are some possible ways of making half an hour of sport:

Gymnastics   20 minutes
Swimming   10 minutes

Volleyball   15 minutes
Athletics   15 minutes

Weight lifting   15 minutes
Basketball   10 minutes
Table tennis   5 minutes

A7 Volleyball, athletics, show jumping, weight lifting and bowls last for a quarter of an hour.

A8 (a) There are 45 minutes in three-quarters of an hour.

(b) There are various ways of making three-quarters of an hour of sport, for example:

Rugby   45 minutes

Skiing   25 minutes
Swimming   10 minutes
Basketball   10 minutes

Show jumping   15 minutes
Volleyball   15 minutes
Bowls   15 minutes

A9 (a) Sam will use 30 minutes of tape.
(b) Pam will use 45 minutes of tape.
(c) Khalil will use 1 hour of tape.
(d) Leon now has 15 minutes of tape left.

Checking and supporting

The rectangular block provides a tangible 'model' of one hour. However it is important that fitting the cards does not become merely a jigsaw puzzle with no thought given to the relationships between the numbers; question **A2** is included as a check on this: if a pupil has difficulty with this question you may need to spend more time talking one-to-one about how lengths of time combine.

From question **A3** onwards a circle is used to represent an hour and this may help reinforce, or be reinforced by, minutes to the hour and minutes past the hour on a clock face.

Page 10 **B Buying blank videotapes**

Video tape and the idea of fitting a series of programmes on a tape should be familiar to most pupils.

Teacher-led discussion

Discussion could centre on the different E numbers available: many pupils may not have realised the relationship between the length of a tape and its E number (though this has been complicated by the long play facility on some machines, which doubles the playing time available).

B1

Length of tape in hours	Length of tape in minutes	Type of tape
2	120	E120
3	180	**E180**
4	240	**E240**

B2 Half an hour of tape is left blank.

B3 (a) He will use 3 hours of tape.
(b) 1 hour of tape will be left blank.

B4 45 minutes (three-quarters of an hour) of the tape will be left.

B5 He can record 6 hours of TV.

Checking and supporting

If difficulties arise in working out how much spare time is left on the tapes in questions **B2**, **B3** and **B4** it may help if you sketch clock-face circle diagrams of the kind on page 8 (for example, one-and-a-half circles to represent a one-and-a-half hour tape).

Extension work

You could consider work on planning and recording a tape on the basis of actual television listings, with pupils perhaps even setting the video themselves (though this may involve the complication of the 24-hour system, which is not met until *Book A3*).

Page 11 # Grouping and multiplication

This chapter aims to reinforce understanding of multiplication as it arises out of equal groups. Work is restricted to multiplication by 2, 3, 4, 5 and 10 and the intention is that pupils should learn these multiplication facts. The pupil's book does not provide practice with extending the 2 times table, so this should be included in teacher-led work, for example by asking about the value of small quantities of 2p coins. You can also introduce the ideas of even and odd numbers at this point. This chapter carefully builds up the demand. Sometimes the groups of objects are visible to the pupil, so the complete set of objects can be counted as a check; at other times pupils will have to rely on their knowledge of multiplication facts.

Further work on multiplication is provided in **Multiplication bingo** later in *Book A2* together with the multiplication card games described on pages 70–71 of this guide. The topic is picked up again in **Cafe** in *Book A3*. It is also important to provide oral practice with multiplication. Count-round games will help ('Up from 4 in 2s' or 'Down from 30 in 3s') though pupils must be able to recall multiplication facts at random as well as by 'counting on'.

Classroom organisation

Pupils can work individually.

Before you start

Each pupil needs worksheets **A2–5**, **A2–6** and **A2–7**, scissors and glue.

A Beads and dots

This is a relatively formal unit of work but the context of jewellery should make sense to the pupil as one in which patterns are likely to occur. The pupil is encouraged to become less dependent on simply counting but has the visual image to fall back on when necessary. Worksheet **A2–6** focuses on building up the 2, 3, 4 and 5 times tables.

A2–5 ▶ A1 (a) 5 groups of 3 makes 15 beads altogether. $5 \times 3 = 15$

(b) 2 groups of 3 makes 6 beads altogether. $2 \times 3 = 6$

(c) 3 groups of 5 makes 15 beads altogether. $3 \times 5 = 15$

(d) 4 groups of 5 makes 20 beads altogether. $4 \times 5 = 20$

(e) 4 groups of 2 makes 8 beads altogether. $4 \times 2 = 8$

(f) 3 groups of 3 makes 9 beads altogether. $3 \times 3 = 9$

(g) 2 groups of 4 makes 8 beads altogether. $2 \times 4 = 8$

(h) 5 groups of 5 makes 25 beads altogether. $5 \times 5 = 25$

A2–6

A2 (a) $1 \times 5 = 5$ (b) $1 \times 3 = 3$ (c) $1 \times 4 = 4$ (d) $1 \times 2 = 2$
          $2 \times 5 = 10$ $2 \times 3 = 6$ $2 \times 4 = 8$ $2 \times 2 = 4$
          $3 \times 5 = 15$ $3 \times 3 = 9$ $3 \times 4 = 12$ $3 \times 2 = 6$
          $4 \times 5 = 20$ $4 \times 3 = 12$ $4 \times 4 = 16$ $4 \times 2 = 8$
          $5 \times 5 = 25$ $5 \times 3 = 15$ $5 \times 4 = 20$ $5 \times 2 = 10$

Page 11

A3 (a) $4 \times 2 = 8$ (b) $5 \times 4 = 20$
     (c) $3 \times 5 = 15$ (d) $2 \times 5 = 10$
     (e) $2 \times 3 = 6$ (f) $3 \times 4 = 12$
     (g) $5 \times 5 = 25$ (h) $4 \times 5 = 20$

Page 12

B Packed in threes

This practises the complete 3 times table.

B1 He sells 30 eggs.

B2

Number of boxes	Number of eggs
0	0
1	3
2	6
3	9
4	12
5	15
6	18
7	21
8	24
9	27
10	30

Page 13

B3 (a) 6 balls   (b) 9 balls
     (c) 18 balls   (d) 21 balls

B4 4 boxes contain 12 balls.

B5 (a) 12 darts   (b) 15 darts
     (c) 24 darts   (d) 27 darts

B6 He will need 7 boxes.

B7 (a) 9 tapes   (b) 21 tapes
     (c) 12 tapes   (d) 27 tapes

B8 They need 3 packs.

Page 14   ## C Packed in various ways

This extends the context used in section B into situations in which pupils must apply their knowledge of the 3, 4 and 5 times tables.

▶ **C1** (a) 8 balls   (b) 16 balls

C2 (a) 30 disks   (b) 40 disks

C3 (a) 6 balls   (b) 15 balls   (c) 3 boxes

C4 (a) 15 cassettes   (b) 30 cassettes   (c) 4 packs   (d) 7 cassettes

D Multiplication jigsaw

This is a challenging activity which requires pupils to recognise the multiples of 2, 3, 4 and 5. Pupils must not have access to a multiplication grid or the point will be lost (though those who do not know how a multiplication grid works will need to have it explained to them). Remind pupils not to stick down any pieces until they all fit. You could consider photocopying the worksheet onto acetate and then cutting out the pieces so that you – or a pupil – could demonstrate on an overhead projector how to start the puzzle.

×	0	1	2	3	4	5
1	0	1	2	3	4	5
2	0	2	4	6	8	10
3	0	3	6	9	12	15
4	0	4	8	12	16	20
5	0	5	10	15	20	25

Follow-up work

You could encourage pupils to create their own multiplication jigsaw for their partner to solve.

Page 15 **Right-angles** Allow two and a half hours

Links with *Book G1* p.13 **Review: angle**, which also touches on angles of other sizes.

This chapter aims to promote recognition of right-angles as well as to make the pupil aware of how important right-angles are in making and building things.

Classroom organisation

Parts of this chapter could be done individually, but pages 15, 17, 20 and 21 are designed for discussion on a group or whole-class basis. It is also best if the whole class or a group attempts the model on page 16 (worksheet **A2–8**), so that pupils don't think that the failure to make a cube is due to their own incompetence.

Before you start

You need some multilink cubes. Each pupil needs a circle of paper (filter papers used in science and cut-out circles are ideal as they emphasise the right-angle as a quarter of a circle when the paper is unfolded on page 16; alternatively torn-out pieces of paper could be used), worksheets **A2–8** and **A2–9**, scissors and glue. You may need some of the punched strips joined with paper fasteners that are used in earlier SMP 11–16 booklet work. A collection of devices for measuring right-angles, borrowed from school workshops, together with various sorts of angle brackets available from do-it-yourself shops, can provide the basis for valuable practice and discussion.

A Right-angles all around you

Pupils are often surprised to find so many right-angles in the classroom.

Page 16 ## B Why right-angles matter

Pupils make their own right-angle and then have a chance to see that using right-angles offers advantages while deviation from a right-angle can cause problems.

Checking and supporting

It is important to make sure that each pupil has folded the paper right-angle carefully enough to be used as a checking device for later work.

 ### Teacher-led discussion

Checking the corners of the 'net' on worksheet **A2–8** reveals that each involves a slight departure from a right-angle. It is only when pupils try to make the net into a cube that they find these combine to produce major inconsistencies. (Despite this, it was reported during trialling that one boy had successfully stuck his model together!)

Page 17   The photographs (together with the picture of the Empire State Building on the front cover of the book) provide a stimulus for discussion and assignments, and would be a good point at which to let pupils see and experiment with a try-square, a designer's set-square and the various kinds of angle brackets. Some possible approaches are as follows:

■ Where in the neighbourhood can pupils find bricks made into a non-right-angle corner like the one in the top right-hand photograph?

■ Who in the class has needed to cut across a piece of fabric at right-angles? Why was this necessary?

■ Pupils can be encouraged to bring something in that they have made (out of wood for instance) in technology. Were there meant to be any right-angles as part of its design? How accurately were these right-angles in fact made?

■ Are there any buildings in the neighbourhood similar in style to those at the bottom of the page?

■ Most windows have right-angle corners. If you have to order a piece of glass for a broken window, what information do you need to give? What would you have to do if the window did not have right-angle corners?

Page 18   ## C Squares and oblongs

We assume pupils are familiar with the punched strips joined with paper fasteners. If not, you may need to let pupils experiment with some for a while.

We have introduced the concept of an oblong – a rectangle that is not a square. This is to avoid reinforcing the common misconception that a square is not a rectangle. When you think pupils are ready for it, you can if you wish explain that squares and oblongs are different types of rectangles.

In this section pupils could be encouraged to use a set-square as an alternative to their paper right-angle.

C1 A square is a shape with 4 equal sides and 4 right-angles.
    A, C and G are squares.

C2 E and J are oblongs.

Page 20 **D Buildings with unusual shapes**

Pupils are presented with a near-impossible task in fitting normal pieces of furniture in a room that has no right-angled corners. (A room like this actually exists and is used as someone's living room.)

Checking and supporting

Some pupils may have difficulty with the idea of a plan view. If so, you will need to help them get started.

Teacher-led discussion

Discussion about wasted spaces in the problem bedroom could lead to the idea that it is easier to fit rectangular furniture into rooms that have right-angle corners. The pupils themselves may have some stories to tell about arranging furniture in awkward-shaped houses.

The buildings in the photographs lack right-angles for various reasons and can be a source of a great deal of discussion. Here are some suggestions for getting it started:

'Who has seen cottages like the ones at Lavenham in the picture? Where did you see them?'

'Who knows of a circular building? Why do you think they made it circular?'

'Can you think of some other unusual-shaped building in our neighbourhood? What shape is it? Why do you think it was made that shape? Tell me about any features it has. Can anyone draw a plan or a sketch of it?'

In all this work try to use, and encourage the use of, mathematical words to describe shapes. Write the words on the board so that they are a resource that others can use when it is their turn to describe a building.

Page 22 **Cookery cards** Allow up to an hour, excluding the pupils' own tasks at the end

This activity gives practice in sorting and searching a simple database in index card form. The questions have been carefully structured in a gentle incline of difficulty.

Before you start

The pupil needs the set of cookery cards made from worksheets **A2–10**, **A2–11** and **A2–12**.

1   (a) The meal is vegetarian.
     (b) It takes 35 minutes to make it.
     (c) It costs 78p per person.

2 (a) The vegetarian meals that cost more than £1 are:
Veggie burgers, chips and beans, vegetable lasagne and leek and mushroom bake.
(b) Jacket potato and cheese takes the longest to get ready.
(c) Cheese on toast is the quickest to get ready.

3 (a) Beans on toast is the cheapest meal Jim could have.
(b) Pot noodle is the most expensive meal Jim could have.

4 (a) Jacket potato and cheese, cheese on toast, eggs and chips, beans on toast, dhal and chappati and scrambled egg on toast are the meals he would eat.
(b) Cheese on toast, egg and chips, beans on toast, dhal and chappati, and scrambled eggs on toast are the meals Mrs Hammond could make.

Page 23   **5** (a) The pupils' own choice of meals that they can cook.
(b) The meals pupils like, can cook and which cost less than 80p.

6 The pupils' own meals

Checking and supporting

Although this realistic context should be familiar to most pupils, some will be unfamiliar with certain words and phrases for meals. In the interests of pupils' general education, you could spend some time discussing these and giving them opportunities to say them.

Extension

The further ideas offered in 'Some more things you could do with cookery cards' could, if the pupil has a real interest in the subject, lead to quite complex work and even form the basis of a piece of practical coursework.

Page 24 # Clock watching

Links with *Book G1* p.32 **Time**, *Book G2* p.19 **Review: Time** and **Time refreshers 1** and **2** in the *Worksheet masters for the G series.*

A significant number of low attainers are unable to tell the time by their early teens; this often causes them acute embarrassment, which in turn prevents them from seeking help. **Early starters** in *Book A1* was designed to identify any fundamental problems and **Getting it taped** in the present book includes related ideas: you should check that all those who are about to start the present chapter did that work; if some had difficulty with it you should (if you haven't already done so) provide extra support before they move on.

All times in this chapter are in multiples of 5 minutes. It gives practice in reading times from an analogue clock and relating them to their digital equivalents. Having a digital clock or watch available can give pupils a good 'feel' for time passing as they are able to see the minutes numbers 'clicking on' in a way that they cannot on an analogue clock.

Most analogue clocks number the hours but not the minutes. The minute hand guide compensates for this, reassuring pupils about what the minute hand indicates. It can be put over the watches depicted in the materials as well as over real clocks or watches. You can, if you wish, tape one on to the centre of the glass face of a real clock. The device is also cheap enough for pupils to have their own to carry around if they wish. Naturally their dependence on it will reduce as their confidence grows.

Classroom organisation

This can be done individually, so long as you are sure that you will be able to check on, and support, any pupils who are having difficulties.

Before you start

You need to prepare the minute hand guides (made from worksheet **A2–13**). Each pupil needs worksheet **A2–14**. You may need a clock face to provide extra support: the hands of the clock need to be geared, so that pupils see the hour hand moving in conjunction with the minute hand; as we explained in **Early starters** it is cheapest to use a redundant clock. If you are doing the topic with a whole class or a large group you should find it helpful to use the clock face made from **A2–OHP1** on an overhead projector. This includes an enlarged minute hand guide as an optional overlay and can be used at any stage in the course for teacher-led practice in telling the time.

A Getting up early

This concentrates on reading the number of minutes after the hour.

A1 (a) It is quarter past 5   (b) Jane is 15 minutes late.

A2 (a) It is 20 past 5.   (b) Jane is now 20 minutes late.

A3 (a) It is 25 past 5.   (b) Jane is 25 minutes late.

A4 (a) It is 25 to 6.   (b) Jane is 35 minutes late.

A5 (a) It is quarter to 6.   (b) Jane is now 45 minutes late.

A6 (a) It is 10 to 6.   (b) Jane is 50 minutes late.

A7 (a) It is 5 to 6.   (b) Jane is 55 minutes late.

Extra practice

Here or later you can devise count-round games based on time, such as 'Forward from three o'clock, a quarter of an hour at a time'.

Page 26   **B On the day trip**

Some digital watches use the 24-hour system. However we don't make an issue of this here and we anticipate that pupils will use the 12-hour system to fill in the digital watches on the worksheet (though we don't expect the use of a.m. and p.m. at this stage). If some pupils decide to use the 24-hour system, that is of course acceptable!

A2–14

    B1 09:10

    B2 10:30

    B3 12:25

    B4 02:40

    B5 04:55

    B6 06:50

Page 27   **C Ready in one hour**

This section deals with what happens when time moves on by exactly one hour.

    C1 Their pictures will be ready at 10:25 in the morning.

    C2 Her pictures will be ready at quarter to three in the afternoon.

    C3 (a) 10:50 in the morning
        (b) Ten past eleven in the morning
        (c) 3:15 in the afternoon
        (d) Twenty to five in the afternoon
        (e) Twenty-five to one in the afternoon
        (f) 1:20 in the afternoon

    C4 At half-past four

Checking and supporting

If difficulties arise in this section they are best dealt with by actually moving the hands of a clock on by 60 minutes.

Page 28 # Target 30

Links with *Book G1* p.56 **The keyboard game**, which practises subtraction instead of addition, and with *Resource pack B* card 24 **Stepping stones**.

This game is like pontoon, though a total above the target is permissible. It gives practice in mentally adding on single digit numbers up to a total of 30 or so. Pupils have to work independently, because of the need to keep their score secret until the end of the game, and some strategic thinking is needed to decide when to stop.

You can of course introduce a 'twist or bust' variation into the rules.

Before you start
Each group needs a pack of playing cards

Classroom organisation
Pupils play in groups of two or more. It is preferable if all in a particular group have similar competence with mental arithmetic. You may need to help take out the picture cards and, as with all games of this kind, you may need to explain the rules.

Page 29 # Patterns by folding and cutting   Allow two and a half hours

Links with *Resource pack B* card 23 **Symmetry**.

This chapter moves on from patterns with a vertical line of symmetry, established in **Symmetrical letters and masks** in *Book A1* to patterns with a single non-vertical line of symmetry or several lines of symmetry.

Classroom organisation
The work can be done by any number of pupils, but if a large group or the whole class do it together this reduces the number of occasions the materials have to be prepared and offers opportunities for some attractive classroom display work that the class can feel proud of.

Before you start
Each pupil needs worksheets **A2–15**, **A2–16**, **A2–17** and **A2–18**, scissors and glue. You also need one or two plastic mirrors for pupils to pass around, and some sheets of coloured paper about 16 cm square: you can use the kind with the glued back or you can use origami paper which provides the opportunity for some very delicate patterns but can be quite fiddly to mount; some of the sheets need to be cut into a circle, or you can use filter papers instead.

A Patterns with a diagonal fold

A2–15 Imagining the effect of a diagonal fold line or mirror line is commonly found difficult. Worksheet **A2–15** tackles this issue by asking pupils to imagine the outcome of each half design before they unfold it. It is important that they go through this whole process with each shape in turn.

Follow-up work

Pupils can work in pairs using square grids like those on the worksheet: one draws half a design and a mirror line; the other attempts to draw in the other half, then this is checked by folding and cutting.

Page 30 ## B Folding more than once

Making snowflakes is a familiar primary school activity, so we have avoided any mention of them here. We hope that pupils will start to appreciate how patterns are generated and will realise that there is a connection between folding and reflecting.

Checking and supporting

You may need to check that the paper has been folded correctly before pupils start cutting. A possible pitfall is that the pupil cuts away too much of a folded edge and the pattern falls apart.

Page 32 ## C Making a doily

Page 33 Folding into six parts can give rise to some quite surprising patterns. The beautiful cut-paper designs on page 33 offer an excellent stimulus to the pupils as well as demonstrating the intricacy that can be achieved in this craft. Nevertheless a beginner can produce an impressive pattern in a fairly short time.

'They would cut out shapes and really like them and ask "how did I actually do it?" So they had to work backwards…They enjoyed that and I think they got quite a lot from it.'

Checking and supporting

Pupils may need help following the instructions for folding into six and you should certainly check their folding before they start to cut.

Page 34 ## D Finding lines of symmetry

Here pupils are encouraged to use both a mirror and a cutting and folding technique to identify lines of symmetry in named plane shapes. We tell them the total number of lines of symmetry on the worksheets to give them an incentive to keep looking beyond those that strike them as obvious.

A2–16

D1 The dotted line is not a line of symmetry.

D2 The dotted line is a line of symmetry.

D3 The dotted line is not a line of symmetry.

D4 The dotted line is not a line of symmetry.

D5 The dotted line is a line of symmetry.

A2–17

Equilateral triangle	3 lines of symmetry
Square	4 lines of symmetry
Oblong	2 lines of symmetry
Regular hexagon	6 lines of symmetry
Isosceles triangle	1 line of symmetry
Parallelogram	no lines of symmetry
Regular pentagon	5 lines of symmetry

A2–18

Rhombus	2 lines of symmetry
Trapezium	no lines of symmetry
Kite	1 line of symmetry
Trapezium with 2 sloping sides the same length	1 line of symmetry
Arrowhead	1 line of symmetry
Regular octagon	8 lines of symmetry
Six pointed star	6 lines of symmetry

Checking and supporting

Make it clear that finding nearly all of the lines of symmetry is a significant achievement, not failure.

Teacher-led discussion

You can use this activity as an opportunity to revise the shape names that pupils know as well as discussing those that are new to them.

Page 35 # Going halves

Links with *Book G1* p.14 **Money**.

This chapter is about halving an amount of money and being able to relate a group of coins to its value in pounds, both as we write the amount and as it appears on a calculator. **Car boot sale** in *Book A1* may have given you some idea of whether pupils have difficulties with money. This chapter should offer you further opportunities to identify and correct pupils' misconceptions: you will need to observe carefully as they work through it.

The theme of money is picked up again in *Book A3* with work on whole pounds in **Money** and on the addition of pounds and pence and calculator representation in **Cafe**.

Classroom organisation

The work can be done individually, thus limiting the amount of money that needs to be provided. However, it may be better if two or three pupils are working on it at any one time so that the money matching activity can be played as a game, with the benefit of self-checking that this provides.

Before you start

A group of pupils needs the money matching cards made from worksheets **A2–19** and **A2–20**. You also need some coins: real ones are far preferable to token ones.

A Change for £5

Halving is introduced as dividing a group of coins into two groups of equal value. Pupils have to check whether a group of coins can in fact be split in this way.

 Introducing the activity

Most pupils will benefit from using real coins for this section. As you hand them out, make sure that the pupil recognises all the coins before starting.

A1 £2·50

A2 Yes, you could have half without needing more change.

A3 (a) Half is £2·50. You would need to change one of the 20p pieces.
(b) £2·50. No more change is needed.

A4 The pupil's own way of making £5

Checking and supporting

You could ask pupils to check that the coins do add up to £5 in each of the photographs: watch them do this to find out whether they really can add coins; if they have difficulty, then counting up of real coins must be practised before they go further with this chapter. Some pupils may just not realise that counting up coins is usually a lot easier if you deal with all the pound coins first, then the 50p coins and so on.

Page 36   **B Using a calculator**

Pupils are asked to tackle each of these halving problems with coins (or in their head) so that they establish what the answer should be before they use the calculator. This way there is a good chance that pupils will work out for themselves how to interpret the calculator display.

B1 Half of £3 is £1·50.

B2 £1·55

B3 (a) £2·05   (b) £2·25
      (c) £2·30   (d) £2·40
      (e) £2·45   (f) £2·65
      (g) £2·80   (h) £2·81

B4 (a) £3·05   (b) £3·20
      (c) £3·00   (d) £3·12

T   Checking and supporting

Questions **B3** and **B4** contain several of the types of amount that cause difficulty, and should certainly be checked before the pupil goes any further.

Page 37   **C Money matching**   Allow at least 20 minutes

This matching activity should help reinforce the points learned in the earlier sections of the chapter.

Checking and supporting

Pupils should be encouraged to use real coins if they are finding it hard to total the coins depicted in black and white on the coin cards. A pupil who is unsure how a calculator will show the answer £2·50, for example, can be shown the trick of keying in '2·50='.

   Some pupils may need help with the instructions for playing the game with one or two friends: a potential mistake is to forget to separate the coin cards from the small cards before starting to deal.

Follow-up work

Pupils can be encouraged to make up their own games using the cards. It often gives them a great deal of satisfaction and they sometimes come up with novel ideas.

Page 38　**D Halving problems**

Realistic contexts are used here with the amounts no longer restricted to multiples of 5p. Pupils are expected to choose their method of working from those developed in earlier sections. In fact, most pupils will benefit from using a combination of methods, perhaps starting by working mentally, using coins when the mental arithmetic is beyond them and using a calculator to check their answers.

D1 Owen will pay £3·50.

D2 Radio　　　　£7·50
　　　Cassettes　　£10·50
　　　Earphones　　£2·25

D3 They should each have £1·17.

D4 The amount cannot be halved exactly because there is an odd penny to deal with.

Checking and supporting

Question **D4** involves an amount of money that cannot in practice be halved exactly. Check that pupils have not simply divided by two on their calculator and copied down the display: they may not be able to produce a practical solution until they have worked on section E, but they should at least recognise that there is a problem.

Page 39　**E More halving problems**

This suggests a way of dealing with amounts that cannot be halved exactly. Again, pupils may use real coins if they need them.

E1 (a) £2·12
　　(b) £2·12 and £2·13
　　(c) £2·13
　　(d) £1·28
　　(e) £1·28 and £1·29
　　(f) £1·29

E2 Monday: each should pay 60p.
　　Tuesday: one should pay 72p, the other 73p.
　　Wednesday: each should pay 65p.
　　Thursday: each should pay 47p.
　　Friday: one should pay £1·12, the other £1·13.

Page 40 **Multiplication bingo** Allow about 25 minutes

This game for 2 to 4 players follows on from **Grouping and multiplication**
earlier in the book and is intended to provide practice in recalling multiplication
facts. You can of course use your own variations of the rules that are given.

Before you start

Each group of players needs two 0–5 dice, about 30 counters and the set of bingo
cards made from worksheet **A2–21**.

 ### Multiplication card games

The cards for these games are made from worksheets **A2–27** to **A2–30** and
contain all the multiplication facts expected in *Books A1* to *A4* inclusive. They
are intended for multiplication practice at any stage during the use of these
books. Since we are suggesting that pupils become confident with a gradually
increasing set of multiplication facts we have labelled each card with the book in
which it could be first used, so (for example) if you are working in *Book A2* you
could pick out all the cards labelled A1 and A2. The seven games are all variants
of the same idea: choose the game that best suits the confidence of the pupil.

Game 1

Lay some multiplication cards face up on the table in
order like this:

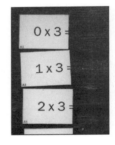

The pupil then sorts through the answer cards to
match each multiplication. Pupils can improve their
speed of matching either by timing themselves or by
racing against one another.

Game 2

Lay out the multiplication cards as in game 1, but shuffle the answer cards and
put them in a pile face down. The pupil turns over one answer card at a time and
matches it to a multiplication card.

Game 3

Shuffle the multiplication cards and lay them out in the order they come off the
pile, so that you get a random column of multiplications. Pupils then *either* sort
through the answer cards to match each multiplication as in game 1 or turn over
one card at a time from a random pile of answers as in game 2.

Game 4

The answer cards are not used for this. Shuffle the multiplication cards and put them in a pile face down. The pupil turns over one multiplication card at a time and says the answer. The pupil puts any that he or she doesn't know to one side and later goes through them to try to learn the answers. Then the multiplication cards are put together and the game is played again.

Game 5

This is like game 4 except only the answer cards are used. Pupils turn over one card at time and have to say a multiplication that matches it.

Game 6

This game for two pupils also needs a teacher, or someone else who can multiply or who has a calculator. Put the multiplication cards in a face-down shuffled pile. The players take turns to turn over the top card. A player who gives the correct answer within five seconds gets to keep it. Failing that the other player gets a chance to respond and keep the card. If no one can answer, the card is put on one side. The player with most cards at the end wins. As an alternative the answer cards are used and players have to give a correct multiplication.

Game 7

This needs two or more players. Both kinds of cards are spread out face down on the table. Pupils take turns to pick up a multiplication card and an answer card. If they match, the player can keep them; if not they must be put back face down. The one with most cards at the end wins.

Page 41   # Weighing it up   Allow at least an hour

Links with *Book G2* p.12 **How heavy?**

This chapter introduces weight through the pupil's own experience of how heavy things feel. It also presents some objects that can be used as points of reference for the magnitude of certain metric weights (like the bag of sugar and the car); you can refer back to these in subsequent work.

Weight appears again in **Make a kilogram** and **Kitchen scales** in *Book A3*.

Classroom organisation
Pupils can work individually or in pairs.

Before you start
You need bathroom scales that weigh in kilograms and a pile of old newspapers. Classrooms usually have most of the items mentioned in activity **1**, but it is worth checking beforehand. We shall remind pupils of the 1 kilogram bag of sugar as a point of reference in future work. It is a good idea to acquire one now as a classroom resource.

Leading the activities
In activity **1** we have deliberately suggested using some items whose size is not directly related to their weight (like the padlock and the empty box), allowing you to make a point about weighing by feel rather than by the impression created by size. It is often difficult to distinguish the heavier of two objects when their weights are similar; pupils should be content to differ in such cases.

In activity **2** the pupil is meant to concentrate on putting familiar objects in order of weight rather than on knowing the weight of each one. You could however ask whether anyone happens to know the weights of any of the objects. Pupils with baby brothers or sisters may remember their birth weights, but these may be known in pounds and ounces rather than kilograms.

Activity **4** leads to the question: what is the greatest weight in kilograms that someone can carry? This is a useful piece of rough and ready knowledge for pupils to have, even though it depends on circumstances and the person's strength.

▶   **3**   The balloon, bag of cotton wool and CD weigh less than 1 kilogram.

Checking and supporting
Activities **4** and **5** call for the use of bathroom scales, but we do not expect the complexities of reading a scale to have been mastered at this stage (though pupils should gain something from watching the scale as the newspapers are added). You may need to give help when pupils come to weigh themselves.

Page 43 # Box curves Allow at least an hour

'I was surprised: I thought there would be more struggling than there was'

This activity reinforces the measuring of whole centimetres needed for **Patterns on tiles** at the beginning of this book. (You should check that pupils did that work before they do this.) The points we made there about the accurate use of a ruler apply here. Once again we have provided a worksheet to establish an accurate outline for the pattern.

Before you start
Each pupil needs worksheet **A2–22** (it is essential that it has been reproduced without distortion).

Checking and supporting
We have kept the instructions brief, so you may need to give some help.

Follow-up work
If any pupils are sufficiently stimulated to want to go on to devise box curve patterns of their own you could spend some time discussing how Bridget Riley uses gradually increasing and decreasing row and column widths to create her effects.

Page 44 # Review: Book A1 and pages 4 to 10

Before you start
Each group of pupils needs worksheet **A2–23**, an 8-sided dice marked N, S, E, W, NE, NW, SE, SW and some counters. Each pupil needs worksheet **A2–24**.

A Compass directions game
The purpose of this game is to reinforce knowledge of the compass directions and their abbreviated forms. Watching the game gives you a good opportunity to judge how well pupils have internalised these ideas.

B Patterns on tiles

A2–24 ▶ The pupil's tile

C Getting it taped

▶ There are many ways of making exactly half an hour of video.

Page 45 **Review:** Book A1 and pages 6 to 21

Before you start
Each pupil needs worksheet **A2–25**, an L-shape made from multilink and a set-square or a paper right-angle.

A Giving change

A1 She gets 22p.

A2 He gets 12p.

A3 He gets 25p.

A4 She gets 70p.

Checking and supporting
If there are problems with these questions you should tackle them before pupils attempt **Going halves**.

B Puzzle it out

`A2–25`

B1 Crossnumber

B2 Number search

C Right-angles

b, e, f, h and m are right-angles.

Review: Book A1 and pages 11 to 27

A Bar chart

▶ **A1** Saturday, probably because of people shopping

A2 Sunday, because a lot of people stay at home

A3 Tuesday, Thursday, Friday and Saturday have more than 400 cars.

B Multiplication patterns

▶ **B1** (a) 8 cartons　　　　(b) 12 cartons　　　　(c) 16 cartons

B2 She will need to buy 5 packs.

C Clock watching

▶ **C1** (a) Ten past seven　　　　(b) Half-past three
　　　(c) Twenty to five　　　　(d) Five to seven

C2 (a) 7:10　　　(b) 3:30　　　　(c) 4:40　　　　(d) 6:55

Review: pages 15 to 34

Before you start

Each pupil needs one copy of worksheet **A2–26**, scissors, an L-shape made from multilink and a set-square or a paper right-angle.

A H-puzzle

Links with *Resource pack B* card 11 **Add ups**, which is easier if the pupil has each number on a small piece of paper that can be tried in different positions.

A2–26 ▶ There are these seven basic solutions (each of which has eight variants produced by reflection or rotation):

B Right-angles

B1 Oblong

B2 Neither of these

B3 Oblong

B4 Square

C Patterns by folding and cutting

C1 (a) It is not a line of symmetry.
(b) It is a line of symmetry.
(c) It is not a line of symmetry.

C2 The shape has 3 lines of symmetry.

Page 48 # Review: pages 24 to 42

A Clock watching

A1 (a) Her watch shows four o'clock. (b) It is really half past three.

A2 (a) Her watch shows half past six. (b) It is really six o'clock.

A3 (a) Her watch shows quarter past eight. (b) It is really quarter to eight.

B Going halves

B1 Half of £3 is £1·50. You would need to change one 20p coin for two 10p coins.

B2 (a) £1·75 (b) £1·15 (c) £2·55 (d) £2·20 (e) £3·50
(f) You cannot halve it exactly. If you were sharing between two people you could give one person £2·12 and the other £2·13.

C Weighing it up

C1 The bananas are the lightest, then the Christmas cake, then the bucket of water is the heaviest.

C2 The bananas will weigh less than a kilogram.
The bucket of water will weigh about 10 kg.

Book A3

Mathematical themes in this book

An important theme is the use of straight and circular scales to read off or to mark values. **Rulers** involves measuring to the nearest millimetre, a skill which is then practised in **Money**. **Angle art 1** and **Angle art 2** introduce the use of the angle measurer, with **Vertical** requiring measurement of angles to the nearest degree. **We asked 100 teenagers** calls for use of the pie chart scale to measure to the nearest one per cent. **Kitchen scales** involves the reading of a dial marked in kilograms and grams.

The ability to estimate heights continues the measuring theme in **Gardens**, which is a substantial data-sorting activity.

Scales are also present in the work on time, which is another important theme throughout this book: time lines are used for support in a.m. and p.m. and 24-hour time, and are implicit in the work on dates in **Calendar** and **The Hancock family**.

Number work is present in most of the chapters. **Halving recipes** introduces elementary scaling-up and down, **Playing Scrabble** requires some appreciation of the need to do calculations in a certain order and **Cafe** provides practice in multiplication, place value and addition of money with and without a calculator.

Planner table for Book A3 (see p.12)

Links with work in Green and Resource packs	Recommended software	England and Wales	Northern Ireland	Scotland
G1 p.6 **Estimating and scales** section B		AT3 level 3	ATM level 3	Measure and estimate levels C, D
		AT4 level 2	ATD level 2	Organise level A Time level B
		AT2 level 3 AT3 level 3	ATN level 3	Fractions, percentages and ratio level B
		AT3 level 1	ATS level 4	
		AT3 level 3	ATM level 3	Range of shapes level C Angle level D
G1 p.14 **Money** G1 p.20 **Money games**		AT2 level 3 AT3 level 3	ATM level 3 ATN level 2	Measure and estimate level C
		AT2 level 3	ATN level 3	Add and subtract level B Multiply and divide level B
G3 p 50 **Have you the time?** section A		AT3 level 3	ATM level 3	Time level C
		AT4 level 3 AT2 level 3	ATN level 3	Time level C
G2 p.20 **Polygon patterns**	**Rose**, in SMILE: the first 30, draws a mystic rose; good demonstration to stimulate pupils' own drawing work	AT3 level 2	ATM level 3	Range of shapes level C Angle level D
		AT2 level 3	ATN level 3	Multiply and divide level C Range and type of numbers level C Add and subtract level C
		AT3 level 3 AT2 level 3	ATM level 3 ATN level 3	Add and subtract level C
G1 p.13 **Review: angle**	**Angle 90,** in SMILE: the first 30, gives practice in estimating angles up to 90°	AT3 level 5	ATS level 4 ATM level 5	Angle level D
		AT2 level 3	ATN level 3	Time level B
		AT2 level 2 AT1 level 3	ATN level 2	Add and subtract level B
		AT2 level 4	ATN level 4	Fractions, percentages and ratio Display level E Interpret level C
		AT3 level 3	ATS level 4	Range of shapes level B
G3 p.52 **Have you the time?** sections B and C		AT3 level 3	ATM level 4	Time level D
G1 p.8 **Estimating and scales** section C G2 p.8 **Reading scales** G3 p.1 **Weight**		AT3 level 3	ATM level 3	Measure and estimate levels C, D

National references

Book A1 Book A2 Book A3

A very confusing
tape measure

Rulers   Allow at least one hour

Links with *Book G1* p.6 **Estimating and scales** section B.

Patterns on tiles and **Box curves** in *Book A2* gave practice in measuring with whole centimetres. If pupils missed that work, try to fit it in before doing this chapter.

Most of us take rulers for granted, but a careful comparison shows that they vary a great deal. They differ in how they line up the numbers with the graduations and in whether or not they label the 0 mark. Some are marked 'mm' or 'cm' near the beginning of the scale, but some give no unit and it is common to see 'mm' and then have the scale numbered in centimetres. This is unhelpful to pupils who have never gained confidence in measuring.

The chapter goes as far as giving a measurement as, say, '4 cm 7 mm' or '47 mm' but does not tackle decimals.

Measuring in centimetres and millimetres is picked up again in **Money**.

Classroom organisation

This is an extended piece of work that may take several lessons.

For pupils who are confident with measuring it will be a piece of revision. Others who still find difficulty will need to have each stage of the work checked if problems are to be identified and overcome.

Before you start

Check that you have some rulers numbered in centimetres (with millimetre graduations) and some numbered in millimetres. Each pupil will need one copy of worksheets **A3–1**, **A3–2**, **A3–3** and **A3–4**. It is worth checking that these have been reproduced without any distortion (see the note in the reprographics guide on page 13 of this guide). You may need the rulers cut from **A3–OHP1**.

Teacher-led discussion

The purpose of the 'Things to talk about' is for pupils to look carefully at the rulers and to think about what the markings on them mean. Use it to check what they already know. When they have identified the longest ruler ask, 'about how long is it?'. This may tell you whether metric or imperial units come more naturally to the group. If someone says the biggest number is 30, ask, 'Thirty what?' Get pupils to look for a short way of writing 'centimetre' and so on.

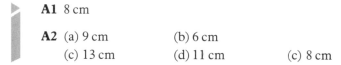
A Measuring in centimetres

This starts with measuring whole numbers of centimetres. We use a ruler that is numbered in centimetres but has millimetre graduations. Some pupils may need to practise first with a ruler that has only centimetre graduations.

> **A1** 8 cm
>
> **A2** (a) 9 cm   (b) 6 cm
>   (c) 13 cm   (d) 11 cm   (c) 8 cm

Checking and supporting

In question **A2** check that pupils have picked out a ruler numbered in centimetres. Also check that they are putting the 0 mark accurately on the end of each line.

Page 5 | ## B Centimetres and millimetres

We use this 'mixed number' approach (5 cm 3 mm) so that pupils can measure lengths that are not whole numbers of centimetres, while producing results that they can relate to their earlier work with whole centimetres. Check that they are writing their results correctly before they get too far with the worksheets. Here, or at other stages in the chapter, you can use an overhead projector to use and discuss the transparent rulers provided on **A3–OHP1**: this has the advantage that everyone in the class is for once looking at the same design of ruler. Cut the rulers out and use them to measure flat objects placed on the projector or drawn shapes. We have included some of the quirks found on real rulers. (The graduations on a real ruler don't show up on an OHP screen because the flanges act as lenses.)

Allow a margin of error of ± 1 mm in the answers.

A3-1

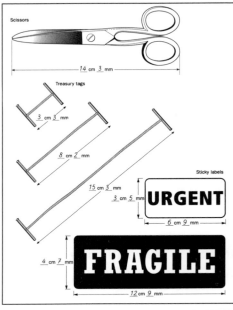

A3-2

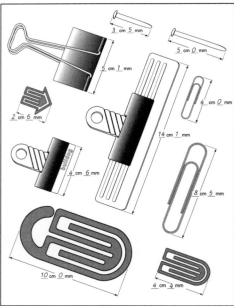

Checking and supporting

We discovered that many pupils did not know what dimensioning arrows are for (one girl measured each half of a dimensioning arrow separately), so we included the photograph of the scissors being measured. Even so, take the opportunity to talk about them: they are a way of saying 'The length from here to here is...'

Page 6 ## C Just using millimetres

Leading the activity

You may need to explain that a millimetre is the distance between 'little marks', not the 'little mark' itself. After pupils have done worksheets **A3–3** and **A3–4** get them to compare their answers with those on **A3–1** and **A3–2**. Use the discussion to draw out the relationship between, say, 3 cm 7 mm and 37 mm. Differences between the two measurements may arise from reproduction problems or inaccurate measuring.

A3–3

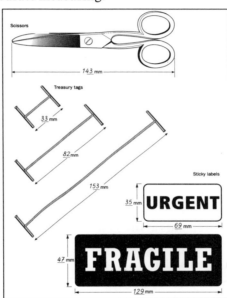

A3–4

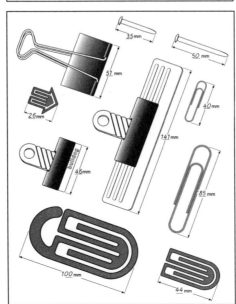

D Inches

This could give rise to some informal discussion of fractions.

E Finding the 0 mark

Measuring pictures of objects in the earlier sections is not the same as measuring the objects themselves, especially as we have made things easy by providing dimensioning arrows.

It is well worth getting together a diverse collection of rulers and measuring tapes like the ones on this page and from time to time asking pupils to measure some real objects, checking that they are lining up the 0 mark accurately and reading off the length with care. Stress the importance of accuracy. You could ask whether anyone knows a true story of something going wrong because a length wasn't measured accurately enough.

▶ The pupil's explanations of where the 0 mark should be.

Gardens   Allow at least two and a half to three hours

This is a planning exercise in which pupils have to sort data to comply with several requirements at the same time.

Classroom organisation
This extended piece of work is best done as a whole group activity. We hope it will be enjoyable and yield some attractive work for display. It is mathematically demanding, though, so be ready to spot problems of understanding and to provide support where needed.

Before you start
Each pupil needs a copy of worksheet **A3–5** and two copies of worksheet **A3–6** (they can be on both sides of a single sheet), a pair of scissors, a sheet of plain paper and access to some felt-tip pens or crayons. It is worth having a couple of seed merchant's catalogues around for extra ideas in section B.

Pages 8–10 | Gardens

T   A Choosing flowers

Teacher-led activities

Once pupils have coloured the flower pictures and cut out the flower labels from worksheet **A3–5** it is worth them doing one or both of the following short activities before starting to sort flowers on worksheet **A3–6**.

The first is a check on their ability to visualise heights. Ask pupils in turn to pick one label, to say the flower's height in centimetres and to stand in front of the group and show with their hand how high the flower will grow. The others must say whether the height indicated is too high, too low or about right. The idea is only to use a ruler as a last resort!

The second activity familiarises them with sorting the cards according to just one attribute, for example,

'Sort the labels into different colours, one pile for blue, one for red and so on…'

'Now make a pile of tall flowers, a pile of short flowers and a pile of medium height ones.' (There shouldn't be too many problems about what counts as tall if the first activity has been effective.)

A3–6 ▶ The pupil's own flower layouts for May and August on two copies of the worksheet.

Checking and supporting

'The group struggled with how the garden would look in May but perseverance paid off.'

Make it clear that a particular flower can be used more than once in the garden.

Some pupils may not know the sequence of names of months or be confident about the seasons of the year they fall in. This work doesn't depend heavily on such knowledge, but it may give you an opportunity to diagnose problems and plan remedial work before they meet the calendar work that begins with **Calendar** in *Book A3* and continues with **Pepper the guide dog** in *Book A4*.

Page 10   ### B Design a garden

Pupils now have a chance to design the garden itself before deciding where to put flowers. They need only produce a rough sketch (an important form of communication), not an exact plan or artistic masterpiece (though some may surprise you!).

▶ The pupil's own garden design.

Page 11 **Halving recipes**

Before you start

As a homework exercise in preparation for questions **3** to **5** you can ask pupils to find a recipe for something they like to eat or to cook . Emphasise that they will need to find out how many people the recipe serves.

Leading the activity

Before pupils turn to the page, explain that they will be looking at a recipe that shows the quantities of food needed for six people and will have to work out how much to use to feed three people. Ask them how they will do it. The answer may not be obvious: this is a broader use of halving than that in *Book A2* **Going halves** which was restricted to sharing between two people. If you get the answer 'Halve it', make sure the whole group understands *why* they will be halving.

Ask them to turn to the page. Point out that the recipe is in two parts, each consisting of some ingredients followed by some instructions. Take the opportunity to discuss how heavy 100 g is (remember the CD in its box in *Book A2* **Weighing it up**?); the abbreviation 'g' for gram may need revising. You could also take the opportunity to find out who knows what °F and °C mean (though there is no need to pursue the topic now unless it seems natural to do so).

Where recipes that they have brought for questions **3**, **4** and **5** are expressed in ounces it may be best just to do the halving in ounces. There may also be the problem of odd numbers of eggs.

Adapting recipes is a useful skill (related to estimating quantities for do-it-yourself work). But stress that it has to be a rough way of thinking: recipes (and labels on packaged food) may or may not be generous when they state how many they serve, and people's appetites vary. If you had a recipe for six people and needed to feed five it might make sense to follow the recipe just as it is.

1 1 large cooking apple
25 g sultanas
25 g sugar
Small pinch cinnamon

2 100 g flour
50 g butter
40 g sugar

3, 4 and **5** Answers from the pupil's own recipes

Follow-up work

You can extend the work to doubling recipes.

Page 12 **Horizontal** Allow at least an hour

In the kind of practical geometry used by builders and do-it-yourselfers, ideas like horizontal and vertical are crucially important. We deal with them first before going very far with the concept of angle. The chapter **Vertical**, later in the book, is in a similar vein.

Classroom organisation

This needs careful planning because different approaches are needed at different points: section A is best done by pupils working in small groups; in section B, checking with a spirit level needs to be done in ones and twos but the number of pupils involved at any one time will be limited by the number of spirit levels available; page 13 and section C on page 14 are best used for teacher-led discussion.

Before you start

You need a table tennis ball, marble or round coin, at least one spirit level, a beaker of the kind used in science half-filled with water. A lemonade bottle filled with water is useful for section B.

A Getting things level

Leading the activity

Before the pupils come in find a small table and check whether it is level.
Ask pupils whether they think the table is level. Gather in answers.
    'How do you know?'
Discuss answers.
    'Can you think of a way of making sure?'
The suggestion of a spirit level might come up at this stage. Affirm it and explain that we will be talking about it later; ask what we could use if we did not have a spirit level.
    Ask pupils to look at the instructions for using a table tennis ball. Get them to try using the method.
    They should conclude that a level table *is* level. Put a book under one leg and get them to check whether it is level now.
    'OK, so it's not level, but what else is wrong with it?'
Try to draw out the idea that it wobbles, it's not stable.
    'What can you do to stop it wobbling?'
They are likely to suggest putting another book under another leg.
    'Under which leg?'

Place the book and establish whether the table has stopped wobbling. Get them to check whether it is level. Get them to continue adding books (of differing thicknesses if necessary) until the table is stable and level.

If the table is unlevel to start with, the discussion can go the same way but you will not need to put a book under one leg to give it some wobble.

Extension

Ask what they can say about the direction the table tennis ball goes in.

'What does it mean if it goes towards the middle of one end of the table?'

'What if goes towards one corner of the table?'

Ask about using other objects besides a table tennis ball.

'Which object is best for telling you that the table is slightly unlevel?'

'Why do you have to be careful if you use a coin?'

B Using a spirit level

For any pupils who can get access to a spirit level at home this could be a homework activity.

A lemonade bottle filled with water, but with enough air left in to create a bubble, makes a good visual aid to provide an animated version of the three spirit level photographs at the beginning of this section.

Page 13 **Teacher-led discussion**

The photographs on page 13 are intended to stimulate discussion. You can ask why each line or surface has to be horizontal; what would happen if it were not? You can also ask about how to get things horizontal: some pupils may know how bricklayers make sure that courses of bricks are horizontal; others may have adjusted the level of a new fridge in exactly the way a pool table is levelled. We asked a billiard table specialist whether he knew any true stories of important games that had run into trouble because the table wasn't level: but he said 'No, it just doesn't happen: they have to be level.'

C Looking at liquids

These questions are best teacher-led.

C1 The water stays level.

C2 She tilted the mould as she poured in the liquid jelly. After this had set she tilted it to another angle for another coloured jelly, and so on.

C3 We hope you enjoy discussing this.

C4 The slope is to let water drain off.

Page 15　# Angle art 1　Allow at least an hour so that pupils can colour in carefully

The main aims are to encourage familiarity with angles and circles, and to give practice in mathematical drawing skills. **Angle art 2**, later in the book, gives more practice of the same kind.

Classroom organisation

This is best done as a whole-group activity and can lead to a good classroom display.

Before you start

Each pupil needs a piece of plain paper (at least 14 cm square) and access to compasses, an angle measurer and felt-tip pens.

In the photographs we have shown Triman safety compasses being used. At the time of writing we think they are the most effective educational device for drawing circles: they are safe, not expensive, pupils with limited dexterity succeed with them and – importantly – the radius setting is visible as a reminder of the defining characteristic of the circle being drawn. A 25 centimetre version is available as well as the short version shown here.

◆T Leading the activity

Check that pupils know what the small parts round the outside of the angle measurer are called. It is easy to mark round in 10-degree steps, because those are emphasised on the angle measurer. But try to ensure that pupils are not just marking on auto-pilot, that they appreciate they are effectively counting in 10s. We haven't used the ° symbol for degrees here (or in **Vertical** later in *Book A3*) preferring to give pupils plenty of exposure to the word spelled out in full at this stage.

For colouring the pattern, felt-tip pen looks better than crayon.

Page 16 # Money Allow about two to two and a half hours

Links with *Book G1* p.14 **Money** and p.20 **Money games**

The work on real notes is designed to develop skills of observation and measurement. Measurement to the nearest millimetre was introduced for the first time in **Rulers** at the beginning of *Book A3*, so you should check that pupils did not miss that. The game 'Coins and notes' aims to help with place value.

Classroom organisation

Because of the need to have some real bank notes available this chapter is best done by only two or three pupils at a time, who can then play the 'Coins and notes' games together. Alternatively, you might consider setting the questions involving real notes as a homework activity.

Before you start

You will need to make sure you have a £5, a £10 and a £20 note ready for the lesson. Each pupil needs access to scissors and crayons or felt tip pens for designing their own £10 note. For the game each group of pupils playing needs a dice, a counter for each person, about £100 in plastic token pound coins (you can buy these in large quantities, without all the other coins, quite cheaply from educational suppliers), the game board made from worksheet **A3–7** (preferably enlarged to A3 size), about 15 token £10 notes (those the pupils designed or some made from five copies of worksheet **A3–8** reproduced on to buff or peach paper).

At the time of writing, the symbols to help partially-sighted people were only printed on Bank of England notes. If you are teaching in Scotland or Northern Ireland you will need to get hold of English notes if you want the pupils to include the symbols in the table for question **6**. In fact it makes an interesting extension of the table to measure and record the dimensions both of your local notes and the Bank of England ones.

Leading the activity

There is a lot of scope for discussion here about what makes a note hard to forge. In question 7 you could give a 'design brief' for the £10 note that the pupils have to design: one teacher stimulated some very interesting work by asking them to design a £10 note 'for the future'.

1 We use coins more often.

2 Coins are more hard-wearing.

3 The date from the borrowed £10 note.

Page 17 4 The two serial numbers on a particular note are the same.

5 They are different.

6	Note	Height	Width	Symbol
	£5	6 cm 9 mm	13 cm 6 mm	●
	£10	7 cm 5mm	14 cm 1 mm	◆
	£20	8 cm 0 mm	14 cm 8 mm	■

7   The pupil's own design.

Page 18 Playing Scrabble®

This requires pupils to think what they are doing when they combine addition with multiplication. They need to see the difference between doubling or tripling a letter then adding, and adding then doubling or tripling the total. The last picture calls for doubling a letter score, adding then doubling the total!

Classroom organisation
This is suitable for whole-class or individual work.

Before you start
It is worth having a real Scrabble set available, both to clarify how the scoring works and to allow pupils to play games if they want to.

1   BREAK   scores 11

2   WELL   scores 7

3   CLEAR   scores 8

4   CLAW   scores 14

5   CAKE   scores 16

6   ELBOW   scores 20

7   GATE   scores 10

8   GATES   scores 14

Checking and supporting
You will need to keep a careful eye on pupils doing this work. It is all too easy for them to get the wrong idea and learn nothing from it.

Extra practice
Playing a real game with a simple dictionary to hand can help with arithmetic as well as with spelling and vocabulary.

You can reinforce the order of operations idea by doing work on money: the cost of 'fish and chips twice' is different from that for 'fish and two lots of chips'.

Page 20

a.m. and p.m.

Links with *Book G3* p.50 **Have you the time?** section A.

This continues the careful progression of work on time. You should ensure that pupils have done the work on time in *Book A2* and that any problems identified there have been dealt with. **24-hour times**, later in the book, takes the topic further.

Classroom organisation

This is suitable for whole-class or individual work.

A When exactly do you mean?

The aim here is that pupils should become familiar with the time line for the day and should be able to use it to deal with questions about a.m. and p.m.

Teacher-led discussion

A discussion of the following kind could come before or after pupils have done the written work.

Ask pupils to recall what they have done earlier in the day.

'About what time did you do that?'

'Was it a.m. or p.m.?'

Ask them to say what they expect to be doing later in the day.

'What time will it be when you do that?'

'Will it be a.m. or p.m.?'

Similarly you could ask them what they did at the weekend or what they plan to do next weekend.

Pupils could produce their own 24-hour time line, labelled with a.m. and p.m. times and label it with things that they do throughout the day.

A1 One will be there at 8 a.m., the other at 8 p.m.

A2 (a) 7:45 p.m.　　(b) 6:30 a.m. to 8.30 a.m.　　　　(c) 11:00 p.m.
　　 (d) 1:00 p.m.　　(e) 7:00 p.m.　　(f) 4:30 a.m.　　(g) 2:00 a.m.

Page 21

A3 (a) morning　　(b) afternoon　　(c) evening
　　 (d) afternoon　 (e) evening　　 (f) morning

A4 (a) 10:30 a.m.　　(b) 6:15 p.m.　　(c) 1:15 p.m.　　(d) 9:30 p.m.

B Using a clock

Some of these depend on the ability to read an analogue clock.

B1 (a) 2:30 p.m.   (b) 1:00 p.m.   (c) 9:15 p.m.   (d) 3:30 p.m.
      (e) 7:45 p.m.   (f) 10:45 p.m.   (g) 9:50 a.m.   (h) 12:35 p.m.

B2 Just after noon or mid-day.

Checking and supporting

Try to include some practice in *saying* a.m. and p.m. times. Point out that we don't say things like 'One o'clock p.m.', we just say 'One p.m.'

Many people (including adults) are confused about the idea behind question **B2**. If a problem arises, refer pupils back to the diagram on page 20.

Page 22 # Calendar

Many pupils lack confidence in the use of a calendar, even though it is important for self-organisation. This chapter provides gentle practice. **The Hancock family**, later in *Book A3*, deals with the use of numbers to represent years; **Pepper the guide dog** in *Book A4* contains more work on days of the week.

Classroom organisation

If enough pupils need to do the work in this chapter it is best done by the whole class or a group, so that you can introduce some discussion on the use of calendars.

Before you start

It is a good idea to have a current calendar available: a large wall-hanging one is suitable for question and answer work with a small group. You can also use slide **A3–OHP2**.

Introducing the topic

The 'something to talk about' should be teacher-led. At this stage of the lesson try to check whether pupils are familiar with '2nd' as a short way of writing 'second', '31st' as a short way of writing 'thirty-first' and so on. If not, try these kinds of practice:

You say a date ('the second of April') and pupils have to write down the short form.

You write a short form on the board and pupils have to speak it aloud.

You may wish to point out that months can be written as numbers, so 1st October becomes 1/10. In this connection, some pupils may have cheap digital watches where this would be shown US-style, as 10/1.

You can use the top part of slide **A3–OHP2** to discuss some of the points or to deal with some of the questions orally. This slide provides a second month for further practice.

1   1st October 1997 is a Wednesday.

2   4th October is a Saturday.

3   31st October is a Friday.

4   The cement mixer is due back on 13th October.

5   The card gets there on 25th October.

6   The car boot sale is on 5th October.

7   He gets 5 lots of pocket money in October 1997.

Extra practice

You could make up further questions based on the calendar in the book; better still, use a calendar for the current month. There are several suitable contexts, like the date a library book has to be back or when your dry cleaning is ready. An aim is for pupils to realise that when a date is required they can sometimes get an answer by adding a number of days to a date, rather than by counting on the calendar.

In question **5**, about posting a letter, we say that it 'gets there 3 days later' rather than that it 'takes 3 days' to discourage pupils from counting 3 inclusive days (22nd to 24th October). It might be worth trying the wording 'takes 3 days' and dealing with the problem if it arises.

Notice that we have used a calendar with a Sunday to Saturday format. The Monday to Sunday calendar is also common so you could consider setting work based on one.

If some pupils seem to have a very tenuous grasp of dates, they will need to come back to them with frequent practice. It helps to let them take it in turns to write the date on the blackboard at the beginning of each lesson. To start with, the month should be written as a word: carry on like this until everyone is confident about writing the date. Then you can use a number for the month.

Extensions

Ask questions that involve going on to the next line of the calendar.
Try inverse problems:

Misha posts a letter to Karachi on 14th October.
It gets there on 23rd October.
How many days later is that?

Talk about calendars in general.

Does the calendar for October look the same every year?

What about the calendars for other months?

Gardens, earlier in *Book A3*, may have revealed that some pupils do not know the names for all the months or cannot say them in the correct order. Take the opportunity to check that any remedial work done then has had its effect. If not, here is something to be practised now. This may be a good moment to talk about how the numbers of days in the months differ: do pupils know any way of remembering this, like the rhyme?

Page 23 # Angle art 2   Allow at least an hour so that pupils can colour in carefully

Links with *Book G2* p.20 **Polygon patterns**.

Several comments (on page 89 of this guide) about **Angle art 1** apply here too.

Before you start

Each pupil needs a piece of plain paper (at least 14 cm square) and access to compasses, an angle measurer and felt-tip pens.

Introducing the activity

You will need to introduce the idea of marking round in 60 degree intervals: the sequence 60, 120, 180 won't be familiar and you will need to discuss how pupils can get these numbers. Pupils who still find difficulty with this could move the angle measurer round 60 degrees at a time (though this can lead to inaccuracy).

Follow-up work

Pupils could do the same sort of pattern but using 30 degree or 45 degree intervals.

A class display of angle art, produced while we were trialling Amber, prompted Nicola to develop her own ideas, first as coursework for GCSE art, and then as a design for her bedroom wall.

Page 24 # Cafe

This provides varied number practice, including mental multiplication and the addition of money on the calculator.

Classroom organisation
This is suitable for pupils working individually.

Before you start
Some pupils may need real coins. For section D each pair of pupils will need the drinks cards (blue), the meals cards (green) and the sweets cards (yellow) made from worksheets, **A3–9**, **A3–10** and **A3–11**, together with one copy of worksheet **A3–12**.

A Helping in Mrs Owen's cafe

Questions **A1** to **A4** focus on extension of the 2 and 5 times tables. Questions **A5** to **A8** reinforce ideas of place value and grouping in tens, in a similar way to the 'Coins and notes' game on page 17 of *Book A3*.

A1 (a) 8 tables   (b) 16 customers

A2 (a) 16 knives   (b) 16 forks   (c) 16 spoons
(d) 40 sachets   (e) 40 sachets   (f) 40 sachets
(g) 80 sachets

Page 25

A3 (a) 5 tables   (b) 20 customers

A4 (a) 20 knives   (b) 20 forks   (c) 20 spoons
(d) 45 sachets   (e) 45 sachets   (f) 35 sachets
(g) 100 sachets

A5 (a) 50 plates   (b) 70 plates

A6 2 piles

A7 (a) 40 plates   (b) 6 plates are left.

A8 (a) 2 piles   (b) 7 plates are left over.

Page 26 ## B Calculate the cost

Pupils may choose to work mentally, possibly with the aid of coins, but if a calculator is used they should at this stage be keying in amounts in pence.

    ▶ **B1** (a) 75p   (b) 85p   (c) 90p   (d) 90p   (e) £1

    B2 £1·40

    B3 (a) £1·50   (b) £1·65   (c) £1·42   (d) £1·99   (e) £2·50

    B4 (a) 200p = £2·00   (b) 205p = £2·05   (c) 95p = £0·95

    B5 (a) £1·10   (b) 95p   (c) £1·45   (d) £1·75

Page 27   ## C Don't mix pounds and pence!

Here pupils must work on a calculator entirely in pence or entirely in pounds.

    ▶ **C1** (a) £1·75   (b) £1·65   (c) £2·15

    C2 (a) £3·45   (b) £1·10   (c) £1·45   (d) £2·00

Extra practice

Pupils will almost certainly need more practice on this, but it should not all be given in the form of written exercises. One possibility is to have a 'dictation': you read out a list of amounts of money, some in pence, others in pounds and pence, and the pupils, each with a calculator, key in the amounts and check that they get the right total. This is closer to the way we have to work with calculators in real life.

D Cherry's cafe

This simulation of bill totalling gives further practice. It is *not* intended that worksheet **A3–12** should be cut up into separate bills.

Page 28   # Make a kilogram   Allow about half an hour

This aims to help develop a sense of the weights of some everyday objects and to reinforce the fact that 1000 g = 1 kg. It also gives practice in mental addition of multiples of 100 (and some multiples of 50); addition of such numbers may be unfamiliar to pupils, in which case you will need to give some practice before they start the game. This is an important piece of preparation for **Kitchen scales**, later in the book.

Before you start

Each pair or pupil playing alone needs the weight cards made from worksheet **A3–13**.

Page 29 # Vertical   Allow up to three-quarters of an hour

Links with *Book G1* p.13 **Review: angle**.

This introduces vertical as a concept, but goes on to include work on using an angle measurer to obtain angles to the nearest degree.

Classroom organisation
This is best done by the whole class or a group.

Before you start
Arrange to do section A near a notice-board. A group doing it needs a few map pins and a plumb line made from a piece of string with a metal nut tied on one end. If possible get a builder's spirit level. Each pupil needs an angle measurer for section B and a copy of worksheet **A3–14** for question **B3**.

A Judging vertical

The group activity establishes what we mean by vertical. Use the photographs of paper-hanging and trees on the side of a hill as a basis for discussion.

Extra practice
Larger spirit levels of the kind builders use have a second bubble that allow you to gauge vertical. If you have access to one pupils can use it to check whether walls, doors, cupboards and so forth really are vertical.

Page 30 ## B How much does it lean?

Although the photographs of an angle measurer being used on the tower at Pisa and the leaning pub give a clear idea of what is required, pupils may need help positioning, and reading off from, the angle measurer, certainly when they come to measure from worksheet **A3–14**. The work on measuring lengths in millimetres in **Rulers** should have given you an idea of which pupils are likely to require most help with this chapter.

If you need to demonstrate the use of the angle measurer to more than just a few pupils, you may find it effective to do so on an overhead projector. Unfortunately, though, the red markings show up black on the OHP screen.

Allow a margin of error of ± 1 in the answers.

> **B1** The tower leans 5 degrees.

Page 31 **B2** The pub leans 10 degrees.

B3 (a) 14 degrees   (b) 7 degrees   (c) 4 degrees   (d) 11 degrees

98

Page 32 **The Hancock family**

Leading on from earlier chapters on time (most recently **Calendar** in *Book A3*), this is the first piece of work on the system we use to number years. Early trialling of draft materials revealed that low attaining pupils often did not understand this system, in spite of work done in history. In this gentle start to the topic pupils make judgements about the ages of people in a family photo and relate these to their years of birth. The work involves counting on and counting back from specified years; a central aim is that pupils should come to understand the principle that someone who is older than another will have a 'lower' year of birth. Further work on this topic is provided in **20th century inventions** in *Book A4*.

Leading the activity

Before using the photo, try asking a group of pupils to work out who is the eldest or youngest among them. The confusions that emerge in their discussion can make quite a revealing start to the work.

The photo acts as a checking device for pupils most of the time, because, for example, they can judge from her appearance whether it is sensible to conclude that Kate is the oldest or youngest granddaughter.

1   (a) Hayley was born in 1980.   (b) Kate was born in 1978.
    (c) Kate is older.   (d) Kate is the oldest of all five girls.
    (e) Sarah, Claire, Hayley, Helen, Kate

Page 33   2   (a) Simon looks older.   (b) Perhaps about 1982
              (c) Perhaps about 1978

          3   (a) William seems older.
              (b) She is possibly younger than John.
              (c) She looks younger than William.
              (d) She could have been born about 1950.

          4   Pete is older.

          5   (a) in 1985   (b) in 1994

          6   (a) 3rd November 1979   (b) 3rd November 1988

Checking and supporting

Since some of the work depends on pupils' judgements rather than factual evidence, you can learn much about thought processes by asking them why they gave their answers. A pupil's explanation for giving Simon a certain year of birth in question **2** (c) might be:

'Well he is definitely older than Mark.'

'I think he looks about Kate's age, or maybe a year older.'

During trialling, answers to question **3** (d) varied greatly, showing how subjective the task of judging ages is: so allow a wide range of answers to this one, so long as they are consistent and pupils seem able to justify them. Don't, however, be tempted to offer a pupil the justification he or she needs for an obvious unsubstantiated guess. Also during trialling several pupils had to be reminded that the complete dates needed for question **6** have to have three elements, day of month, month and year.

If pupils have persistent difficulties with this work it may be the remoteness of the photo of an unknown family that is responsible. You may also be sensitive to perceptions of pupils who don't have a formal family structure of their own. In such cases you might wish to substitute the approach given under 'follow-up work' below.

Challenge

We found that bringing pupils' own families into the discussion stimulated interest. Clearly a great deal of diplomacy will be needed if pupils are to investigate teachers' dates of birth. However, we found that discovering the real dates motivated pupils to perform quite complex calculations: as well as ordering dates they even worked out the intervals between them.

Follow-up work

You can devise similar questions based on collectors' football cards: these carry birth dates and significant career dates, such as international debuts. (We would have included some of these in the pupil's book, but for the fact that they go out of date so quickly.)

Page 34 # Honeycombs

This involves mental addition as well as providing practice in trying out different possibilities systematically.

Before you start

Each pupil needs a copy of worksheets **A3–15**, **A3–16** and **A3–17**. You may find it useful to photocopy one or more of these worksheets on to acetate for use on an overhead projector during discussion.

  1   Steven's total is 14.

  2   Narinder's total is 15.

A3–15 **3** The pupil's own paths and totals

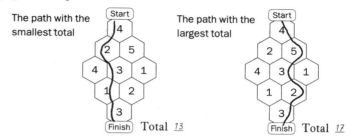

The path with the smallest total — Start, 4, 2, 5, 4, 3, 1, 1, 2, 3, Finish — Total *13*

The path with the largest total — Start, 4, 2, 5, 4, 3, 1, 1, 2, 3, Finish — Total *17*

A3–16 **4** The pupils' own paths and totals

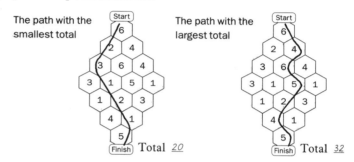

The path with the smallest total — Start, 6, 2, 4, 3, 6, 4, 3, 1, 5, 1, 1, 2, 3, 4, 1, 5, Finish — Total *20*

The path with the largest total — Start, 6, 2, 4, 3, 6, 4, 3, 1, 5, 1, 1, 2, 3, 4, 1, 5, Finish — Total *32*

A3–17 **5** The pupil's own paths and totals

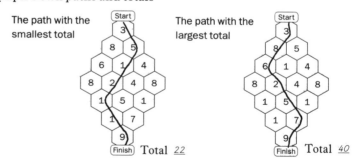

The path with the smallest total — Start, 3, 8, 5, 6, 1, 4, 8, 2, 4, 8, 1, 5, 1, 1, 7, 9, Finish — Total *22*

The path with the largest total — Start, 3, 8, 5, 6, 1, 4, 8, 2, 4, 8, 1, 5, 1, 1, 7, 9, Finish — Total *40*

Page 35 # We asked 100 teenagers

We have used a none-too-serious TV show context for this introduction to percentages. (You might, incidentally, like to point out that these are not the sort of questions to ask in a proper survey: 'Name something you …' seeks neither a fact nor an opinion.) Here the 'base' of the percentage is always 100 teenagers, so no calculations have to be done: the main aim is to make the terminology 'per cent' and 'percentage' familiar and to give pupils practice in the use of a pie chart scale. Work on bases other than 100 is begun in **Percentages** in *Book A4*. Allow a margin of error of ± 1% in marking the answers.

Classroom organisation

The chapter is suitable for individualised or whole class work.

Before you start

Each pupil needs a pie chart scale.

A Collecting the facts

If pupils are unfamiliar with the use of a pie chart scale, you will need to make an input at this stage. If you need to demonstrate its use to more than just a few pupils, you may find it effective to do so on an overhead projector; this is also a good way of leading a question-and-answer session on measuring pie charts.

A1 28 per cent said 'a towel'.

A2 11 per cent said 'goggles'.

A3 11 per cent gave other answers.

A4 The pupil's own answers

Page 36 ## B Measuring pie charts

B1 (a) Music was most popular.
(b) 66 per cent

B2 18 teenagers

B3 10 per cent

B4 6 per cent

B5 Left it at home: 43 per cent
Forgot to do it: 19 per cent
Dog ate it: 11 per cent
Had to go out: 9 per cent
Didn't understand it: 4 per cent
Lost it: 4 per cent
Other: 10 per cent

Page 37 ## C Drawing your own pie charts

C1 The pupil's pie chart

C2 The pupil's pie chart

Page 38 **Four cubes** Allow a half to one hour or possibly more

This is a simple introduction to recognising shapes from different viewpoints.

Classroom organisation

This is best done as an individualised piece of work because of the need for a quantity of multilink cubes.

Before you start

Each pupil needs 52 multilink cubes and some sticky labels with the letters A to M written on them. You can cut them from an adhesive address label or masking tape.

▶ 1 These models are the same.
   A, D and F,   B and L,   E and J,   G, H and M,   C and K

 2 Model I is different from all the others.

 3 A model like this (or its mirror image)

Follow-up work

If pupils have answered questions **1** and **2** confidently with the help of the models they have built, you can (perhaps after a gap of a few days) see whether they are now able to answer them just by looking at the pictures in the book.

Page 39 **24-hour times**

Links with *Book G3* p.52 **Have you the time?** sections B and C.

This follows on from **a.m. and p.m.** earlier in *Book A3*.

Classroom organisation

This could be done on an individualised basis, but doing it as a whole- class or group topic allows you to do oral work based, for example, on the pupil's own day.

T **Introducing the topic**

As well as checking that the ideas of a.m. and p.m. have been remembered, it is a good idea to practice these before doing the chapter:

   Adding on 10, 11 or 12 to a number between 1 and 12

   Subtracting 10 from a number between 11 and 24

   Subtracting 11 from a number between 12 and 24

   Subtracting 12 from a number between 13 and 24

► **1** (a) 15:00 (b) 07:00 (c) 22;00
(d) 17:00 (e) 04:00 (f) 18:30

2 (a) 16:00 (b) 10:00 (c) 20:00
(d) 13:30 (e) 12:00 (f) 13:00

3 (a) 11:00 p.m. (b) 8:00 a.m. (c) 9:00 p.m.

Page 40 **4** (a) 18:00 (b) 13:00 (c) 13:30
(d) 19:00 (e) 22:30 (f) 20:30

5 (a) 8:00 a.m. (b) 4:30 p.m. (c) 8:30 p.m.

Extra practice
The Taskmaster '24-hour clock dominoes' work well.

Page 41 # Kitchen scales

Links with *Book G1* p.8 **Estimating and scales** section C, *Book G2* p.8 **Reading scales** and *Book G3* p.1 **Weight**.

This chapter reviews metric and imperial measures of weight, and gives practice in reading scales marked in grams and kilograms. Check that pupils have played the game **Make a kilogram** earlier in this book.

Classroom organisation
This is best started as an activity with the whole class or a group, to take advantage of the opportunities for practical demonstrations.

Before you start
Each pupil needs a copy of worksheets **A3–18** and **A3–19**. You need a set of kitchen scales to introduce the chapter, and a pound and a kilogram weight if possible. You may need slide **A3–OHP3**.

 A Pounds and kilograms

Use page 41 of the pupil's book to talk to them about the two systems we use for measuring weight. Emphasise that we do not usually need to convert pounds into kilograms or vice versa, because people usually choose which system to use and then keep to it. Every pupil needs to know that a kilogram is heavier than a pound. It is also sometimes useful to know that a pound is roughly half a kilogram (and a kilo is just over two pounds), so you may wish to point this out to some pupils.

A practical demonstration of weighing out (as near as you can) a pound and a kilogram of, say, potatoes or onions can be very helpful.

A1 The pupil's own birth weight

A2 The 1 kilogram weight is heavier.

Page 42 **B The numbers on the scales**

This gives practice in reading the kilograms and grams scale on kitchen scales, using weights that are multiples of 250 g. Here we suggest writing weights as mixed quantities of kilograms and grams, but if pupils realise there are other ways – using only grams, or even decimals – then there is no reason for them not to be supported in doing so.

Introducing the work
You can use slide **A3–OHP3** to lead some whole-class oral work on reading from the scale before pupils answer the questions in the book.

B1 1 kg

B2 4 kg

Page 43 **B3** 500 g

B4 500 g

B5 The pupil's answers on the worksheet

B6 The pupil's answers on the worksheet

Extra practice
Further practice weighing packets on kitchen scales can be invaluable. You may want to make your own worksheets based on the kitchen scales pupils are actually using, especially if the dial on yours is marked in 200 gram increments rather than 250 gram as on our worksheets: try removing the dial and doing a reduced photocopy of it, or sketch it yourself.

C Different scales

You may be able to borrow other sorts of scales from the science and technology departments in your school.

The pupils' own drawings

Page 44 **Review:** Book A2 and pages 4 to 17

A Multiplication

▶ **A1** (a) 12   (b) 15   (c) 10   (d) 8

B Rulers

▶ **B1** (a) 1 cm 6 mm   (b) 1 cm 1mm   (c) 1 cm 3 mm
       (d) 1 cm 8 mm   (e) 2 cm 1mm   (f) 2 cm 4 mm   (g) 8 mm

   B2 (a) 2 cm 1mm   (b) 1 cm 1 mm   (c) 1 cm 8 mm   (d) 1 cm 3 mm

   B3 Opening E fits nut (a).   Opening B fits nut (b).
        Opening D fits nut (c).   Opening C fits nut (d)

C Money

▶ **C1** Jo has £16.

   C2 She gets 40 coins.

   C3 He has £44.

Page 45 **Review:** pages 11 to 22

A Halving recipes

▶ **A1** Filling: 200 g blackberries, 60 g sugar
       Pastry: 150 g flour, 100 g butter, 50 g sugar

   A2 4 people

B a.m. and p.m.

▶ **B1** The pupil's own answers

   B2 (a) 3:30 a.m.   (b) 6:45 p.m.   (c) 7:15 p.m.